WICKED BECOMES HER

*Bette Davis and The Story
Behind 'Wicked Stepmother'*

JOHN WILLIAM LAW

Wicked Becomes Her

*Bette Davis and the Story
Behind 'Wicked Stepmother'*

By John William Law

Aplomb Publishing

Wicked Becomes Her: Bette Davis and The Story Behind 'Wicked Stepmother' by John William Law

Print ISBN: 978-0-9993069-7-0

© 2024 Aplomb Publishing, a division George + William Corporation.

Aplomb Publishing
San Francisco, California

"What occurred was even more tragic because Bette and I had grown terribly fond of each other."

- Larry Cohen, Writer/Director of Wicked Stepmother

"No studio head can make you a star. The audiences made me a star."

- Bette Davis

Dedication

Dedicated to Larry Cohen,
writer and director of *Wicked Stepmother*.
Without him, this book would not have been possible.

Acknowledgments

Thank you to Dennis Constan for editing support, and Thomas Moulton for design assistance and advice. Special thanks to Larry Cohen for background production material and details and the Motion Picture Academy of Arts and Sciences and the Margaret Herrick Library for access to research material.

Preface

"Everybody else gives Bette dinners. I gave her a job."

- Larry Cohen, Writer/Director of *Wicked Stepmother*

Opening Remarks

Her hair is Harlow gold
Her lips sweet surprise
Her hands are never cold
She's got Bette Davis eyes
She'll turn the music on you
You won't have to think twice
She's pure as New York snow
She got Bette Davis eyes

And she'll tease you
She'll unease you
All the better just to please you
She's precocious, and she knows just
What it takes to make a pro blush
She got Greta Garbo's standoff sighs
She's got Bette Davis eyes

She'll let you take her home
It whets her appetite
She'll lay you on the throne
She got Bette Davis eyes

She'll take a tumble on you
Roll you like you were dice
Until you come out blue
She's got Bette Davis eyes

She'll expose you, when she snows you
Off your feet with the crumbs she throws you
She's ferocious, and she knows just
What it takes to make a pro blush
All the boys think she's a spy
She's got Bette Davis eyes

And she'll tease you
She'll unease you
All the better just to please you
She's precocious, and she knows just
What it takes to make a pro blush
All the boys think she's a spy
She's got Bette Davis eyes

She'll tease you
She'll unease you
Just to please you
She's got Bette Davis eyes
She'll expose you

When she snows you

She knows you

She's got Bette Davis eyes

Bette Davis Eyes

Written by Jackie DeShannon and Donna Weiss; recorded by Kim Carnes, 1981.

...

66 She's pure as New York snow," says one iconic line in the song *Bette Davis Eyes*. Recorded by Kim Carnes in 1981, the song spent nine weeks at the top of the Billboard pop music charts, becoming the biggest hit of the year. It was as iconic as the woman it spoke of and carried a star of years-gone-by into 80's pop culture. After Carnes met the legend on which her song was based, she remarked, "She doesn't compromise and doesn't take guff from anybody."

I have been writing books for more than 20 years, after having spent a number of years writing for newspapers and magazines. Though the initial steps or processes to create a book can be similar, the books themselves seem to travel their own paths - and can sometimes come out quite different than intended.

The idea behind this book began back in 2002 when I was writing another book called *Reel Horror*. Published in 2004, *Reel Horror* chronicled a series of horror films that had troubled paths to the big screen. One of the stories I fought to include in that book was a chapter on the making of *Wicked Stepmother*, Bette Davis' final film.

Though *Wicked Stepmother* isn't really a horror film, I wanted to include it for very specific reasons. The film is more a black comedy than anything, and its theatrical release left much to be desired, since it only appeared in a few movie houses before heading straight to video. However, *Wicked Stepmother* is in many ways, a spoof of the horror movies of the 1980s, as well as a tribute to the collection of horror films in which Bette Davis starred in during the latter years of her career. While the film itself can be easily passed over in viewing, the tale behind its making is a fascinating one.

I was working for a newspaper on the east coast at the time of the film's release. Months later, when Davis died, I wrote a small article about the film and the legendary actress, after *Wicked Stepmother* arrived on home video shortly after her death.

Bette Davis abandoned the film early in production and failed to return to complete the project. Davis was so horrified by the way she looked in the rushes that she decided that she could no longer appear onscreen, though she longed to work until the very end. There has been some suggestion that the story and script played a role in her refusal to complete the film. Others suggest that it was simply her disdain for how old and frail she appeared and sounded, coupled with her lacking the stamina to endure the shooting schedule, that drove her exit.

Bette Davis had hoped that by exiting the film she would have spared her public from ever having to witness her performance. However, Larry Cohen, the film's director/producer, had other plans.

Cohen's concept for the film was developed entirely for Bette Davis as a star of horror classics like *What Ever Happened to Baby Jane, Dead Ringer* and others. As star of the vehicle, Davis was the sole purpose for the film to be made at all. Without her the film held no meaning, and Cohen knew this. With a week's worth of footage of Davis in the can, Cohen felt that he could rewrite the script to utilize what footage he had and to complete the film without her. Her name still had value and the money spent on her would not be wasted.

Bette Davis' foray into horror began in 1962 with the release of *What Ever Happened to Baby Jane?* This hit film, and the longstanding feud between Davis and her co-star Joan Crawford have spawned books, films, documentaries and more. The success of the film would drive both actresses to second careers as stars of a host of good and bad horror films. In fact, the popularity of *What Ever Happened to Baby Jane?* would lead many aging actresses to find film roles in cheesy horror movies. Barbara Stanwyck, Olivia de Havilland, Shelley Winters, Debbie Reynolds, Tallulah Bankhead, Lana Turner and others found themselves being terrorized onscreen in hopes of reaping rewards at the box office.

Fascinated by the idea of this phenomenon, I authored *What Ever Happened to Mommie Dearest?* in 2012 on the 50th anniversary of *Baby Jane's* release. Through the career of Joan Crawford, I looked at how the need and desire to keep working would lead a successful leading lady into a career starring in lackluster horror films. Joan Crawford, like Bette Davis, was a poster child for this transition. Crawford was heavily in debt by the end of the 1950s after the death of her fourth husband. She found that he had leveraged her financial future and had left her with nothing. Trained for little else, Crawford did the only thing she could do - she returned to Hollywood.

However, when the roles became harder to come by, she took what work she could. She gambled on *What Ever Happened to Baby Jane?* by personally asking Davis to co-star alongside her, and in getting Robert Aldrich, a director with whom she had worked with previously, to direct the film. She had accepted a smaller salary in exchange for a cut of the box office, and both she and Davis came out as winners when the film succeeded. However, the price that she paid was that most of the work she would do during the remaining 15 years of her life would be horror-related. I started researching the idea of a book on Davis in 2014, but I deferred it to other efforts.

Bette Davis fared better, but it was a slippery slope even for her. Davis outlived Crawford by more than a decade and worked right up to the very end. The films she made during this time left something to be desired, while a few of these later films have stood the test of time. The most memorable of these are the horror films. *Dead Ringer; Hush, Hush ... Sweet Charlotte; The Nanny; Burnt Offerings* and others are regarded as camp classics. Her work in TV fared better, but it is still largely forgotten by those reviewing her lengthy career.

In 2017, the airing of the miniseries *Feud*, starring Susan Sarandon as Bette Davis and Jessica Lange as Joan Crawford, renewed interest in the two Hollywood legends and inspired me to begin this effort again. While projects like these can take years, and other efforts required attention, Bette Davis remained in the back of my mind as I continued to develop the chapters of this book.

Wicked Becomes Her aims to revisit the latter years of Bette Davis' career with specific attention to the collection of horror films that kept her in the public eye, but it weaves the story through the lens of her final film. It was this film - and her sheer determination to keep working - that sheds the most light on the person behind the actress.

There have been many excellent biographies on the life and career of Bette Davis. The attention here is to look at the drive of a movie star, whose desire to maintain an active career was so strong that she would justify a film for no other reason than the fact that her name was on the marquee as its star.

Bette Davis had a career that spanned six decades and offered some of the best performances an actress has ever given. Let there be no attempt to diminish her accomplishments. Success and failure are often intertwined and time has a way of mitigating both. Bette is no more or less a legend for the films that captured her at her best; but it is those films that caught her past her prime, that demonstrate how she could weather the test of time; survive failure; and still remain a legend.

When I started this book, Writer/Director Larry Cohen was still alive. I contacted him about the book during the research phase and while I found him reluctant to revisit the past I was able to acquire some insight from him on his observations and the events that were vital to tell this story. Other interviews and Cohen's writings and notes provided added details on his association with Davis. His insights were instrumental in telling the other side of the story. Invaluable was a copy of his original script that provided insight into the film Cohen originally intended to make - you'll even see sections of it referenced throughout the book as well as images of actual scenes and dialogue. This book is as much a testament to his tenacity and dedication as it is to Bette Davis. Cohen was a brand of filmmaker that thrived on the idea of Hollywood and the living of a dream. While his films were marred by challenges in getting a film produced, they also herald in their ability to find life at all.

Film is about telling stories and good films can only exist by having bad films to illustrate the difference. Cohen made his share of bad films - and some good ones as well. Cohen was as much a writer as he was a director and producer. He likely found himself more successful as a writer. However, to charge Cohen as a lackluster filmmaker limits our ability to enjoy his love of storytelling and his glimmers of success.

While *Wicked Stepmother* might not be considered among Cohen's best endeavors, it celebrates Hollywood and the legends that created a golden era of film that inspired people like Cohen to build their careers.

Cohen had met with Davis prior to her accepting the part. He had expected that she would need to be convinced the film was right for her. However, with a lack of film offers, Davis was eager to find something to do. At the end of the meeting at her home she had her assistant open a bottle of wine. "It was her tradition to offer a toast," Cohen recalled. Bette's toast: "Let's hope we like each other at the finish as much as we do at the start."

- John William Law

Larry Cohen with Bette Davis filming *Wicked Stepmother*.

1

"It began as an effort to help her resurrect her dormant career and ended with the final nail in the coffin of a legend."

- Larry Cohen, Writer/Director of *Wicked Stepmother*

Chapter 1

A Career By the Sum of Its Parts

Weeks before **Wicked Stepmother** *went before the cameras, Bette Davis' bridgework cracked and began to fail her. Eager to get to work and not wanting to delay the picture, "Bette tried to fake it and failed," recalled Larry Cohen. "She could barely get the lines out because of the necessary pauses to readjust the bridge with* *her tongue. For a perfectionist like Bette, this was pure hell. And yet she never leveled with me. If she had, I certainly would have closed down for a month and reshot the early scenes upon her return."*

Cohen believed that when Davis ultimately walked off the picture her only recourse was to place blame on him - her director. "I was willing at the time to take the rap. That was my final gesture of admiration and friendship. After all, I was to blame for getting her into this mess."

...

It was the spring of 1988, on Friday, May 6, that Bette Davis walked off the set of her last film. The film had been in production less than two weeks. Davis had been eager to see the dailies of her work but frustrated at the director's unwillingness to present them to her.

Dailies are the presentation of the raw, unedited footage shot during the making of a film. Traditionally, at the end of each day's filming, the footage captured is developed; synched with sound; and printed to a reel of film or a digital file is stored. Most often the director, key members of the production crew, and sometimes the leading actors have an opportunity to view the early work the next day or at the end of a week. The footage can be a barometer for how a film is progressing and for the quality of the performances and scenes captured. It also can highlight issues and give the director an opportunity to adjust the filming before things veer too far off course.

After receiving Davis' requests to see the dailies for days, Larry Cohen finally agreed to allow his star to view the film he had shot that first week. The director had avoided showing the footage to his star for good reason. He knew the footage was rough. She sounded bad. She looked even worse. Her movements were awkward and it would take serious editing to salvage a performance from his aging star. He had planned to fix as much of this as he could during post-production, but she persisted to the point of breaking down nearly to tears, telling him she had to see her work. He relented and on Saturday, May 7, 1988, Bette Davis saw the result of her work.

Dressed in black and with her personal assistant nearby to support her, Bette sat down in the production offices quietly to watch the footage. It would not go well. "When she showed up at the projection room that afternoon and saw how she looked in the dailies, she became very despondent," recalled Cohen.

Shocked by what she saw on the screen, Davis knew in the back of her mind that her career was over. She had been having troubles with her dentures prior to the beginning of principal photography and her cracked bridge was hard to hide. As she watched the footage she could see her broken and paused speech as she stammered, trying to keep her teeth in her mouth. In her gaunt state, her face and figure appeared weak and frail. Her movements were stiff and awkward, her appearance bordered on horrific. It was difficult for her to watch and she faced a quandary as to what to do. While she had looked bad on film before it had been intentional. As Jane Hudson in *What Ever Happened to Baby Jane?,* it even played in her favor, earning her an Academy Award nomination. However, this time, it was neither the costumes nor the makeup ... it was she.

After viewing the dailies she left with little to say. She immediately booked a flight to New York and made an appointment to see her dentist. If she could correct the problem with her dentures she might be able to resume the picture and salvage her performance. She was being paid handsomely and had signed a contract.

Her dentist's initial examination found that the dental problem was far more serious than fixing just her bridge. She needed to have several teeth extracted, and it would then require him to build her an entirely new set of dentures and fit her carefully.

While the situation might have been unremarkable or ordinary, it was extraordinary to Bette Davis for two reasons. First, at her advancing age and declining health, any form of surgery, including the extraction of teeth, was serious. After a mastectomy and stroke several years earlier, her weight had become a challenge, and maintaining a healthy weight was difficult. She was barely eating enough to stay active. Sustaining herself on a few bottles of nutritional supplements would not be enough, but with surgery in her mouth, it would be all she could consume.

The second, and less public reason, was that her dental issues were not new. It had been a problem that impacted her as a child and later as an adult. Her mother and she both suffered from a disease called Osteomyelitis.

...

It was back in 1922 when Bette's mother, Ruthie Davis, scraped together enough money to send her daughters Bette and Bobby to summer camp in Lovell, Maine. Camp Mudjekeewis was a breath of fresh air - literally - for the city girls, where they enjoyed a summer of swimming, canoeing, and horseback riding.

The downside was that the cost of the camp left Ruthie short of funds to keep the family living in their small apartment. So, the trio moved out of New York to East

Orange NJ, after an acquaintance had recommended a more affordable option. Moving into a boardinghouse, Ruthie and Bobby shared the bed while Bette slept on a small cot beside them in the tiny single room that they now called home.

About two months after moving to East Orange, Ruthie became sick. Feverish and with an aching jaw, she went to a dentist for what she thought was a toothache. The doctor diagnosed Osteomyelitis - a severe infection - in her jawbone.

Osteomyelitis is an infection of the bone when harmful bacteria invade the bone. The infection can travel through the bloodstream or spread from nearby tissue. In some cases the infections can begin in the bone itself. While it can occur in both children and adults, osteomyelitis can differ in symptoms and impact. In children, Osteomyelitis often affects the long bones of the legs and upper arms, while in adults it is more common in the bones that make up the spine and vertebrae. Osteomyelitis of the jaw is defined by the presence of exposed bone in the mouth. Inflammation of bone cortex and marrow can develop in the jaw, resulting in a chronic infection.

Long considered incurable, Osteomyelitis can now be successfully treated with antibiotics. In severe cases, surgery to remove parts of the bone that have been killed by the infection is sometimes necessary. Surgery is followed by strong doses of antibiotics that are delivered intravenously to kill any infection. While treatment today can typically take four to six weeks, in the past recovery was often lengthy and painful.

After cleaning out the infection and stitching her up with twenty stitches, her dentist sent Ruthie home where she collapsed on the sidewalk before ever making it inside the boardinghouse. Neighbors helped get her inside. Responding to a call, her sister Mildred arrived a short time later to collect her, relocating Ruthie and her daughters to be closer to her in Newton, Massachusetts. They found another boardinghouse and life resumed as expected. It was not a happy time for young Bette.

Osteomyelitis would be a recurring theme in Bette Davis's life. From that first introduction to the infection with her mother's illness, when she was just fourteen, Bette would later suffer from Osteomyelitis herself.

Bette encountered the pain and suffering first-hand in 1952. It was a time when film projects were sporadic and she was offered a chance to return to the stage. After Davis' Oscar-nominated performance in *All About Eve* as a dedicated stage thespian, the timing was right. She had had a long history of performing on and off Broadway before live audiences, and it was the perfect moment to usher her return to live performing. Producer Mike Ellis offered her the lead in a musical review called "Two's Company." Bette eagerly accepted.

With sketches by Charles Sherman and Peter DeVries, and music by Vernon Duke, and most of the lyrics came from Ogden Nash and Sammy Cahn, the show consisted of comedy and musical sketches about show business. Davis would deliver song-and-dance routines and commentary that focused on life in the theater, on film, and in TV.

In October 1952 the play opened at the Shubert Theatre in Detroit to test the material before heading to Broadway. Midway through the production Davis collapsed from exhaustion, but mustered the strength to soldier on. Initial reviews were good, but when the show moved to Pittsburgh, audience response was less enthusiastic and the producers began tightening the play and reworking the song and dance numbers to pick up the pace. After hitting Boston the show was still being reworked - with actors being recast; sketches dropped; and musical numbers retooled. Bette was still not feeling her best.

With Davis ill, the Broadway opening was delayed from December 4 to December 15, 1952 when it finally opened at the Alvin Theatre on West 52nd Street. Even with

90 performances to sold-out audiences, "Two's Company" garnered mixed reviews at best. Bette continued to suffer from exhaustion and doctors struggled to find the cause.

After her wisdom tooth had become infected, it was discovered that she too, like her mother, suffered from osteomyelitis of the jaw. Immediate surgery was required that forced Davis to drop out of the show. Rather than replace the star, the producers would close "Two's Company," losing $320,000 in the process due to cancelled performances.

With surgery came the extraction of several teeth. A set of dentures were created for Bette that would allow her to talk and eat normally. It would also require weeks of recovery as she dealt with the pain not only from the infection but also from the surgery to repair the damage. She also had to learn how to live with dentures, and it would change her speech patterns. Her distinctive stilted way of talking developed as she got used to talking with dentures became something she would live with for the rest of her life.

Dental issues related to her earlier bout with osteomyelitis reappeared in 1961. Bette was again appearing onstage, this time at the Royale Theatre on West 45th Street in New York. While in the stage production of "Night of the Iguana" she started having difficultly with her mouth. Along with Margaret Leighton and Patrick O'Neal, Bette had signed on to four months of pre-sold bookings, but she was a bundle of raw nerves and anxiety over the role. While Leighton came away with a Tony Award for Best Actress, Bette wasn't even nominated. The play was selected the best American play of 1961-62 by the Critics' Circle; but by then, Bette had bowed out.

Bette immediately went to see her dentist when she began to notice the problems. She feared a repeat of the 1952 episode, but fortunately the situation wasn't as dire as before. "I had to reposition her teeth because they were moving inside her mouth," said her dentist, Dr. Ivan Prince. "They were spread out all over."

Prince recalled that as he worked on her she expressed how much fear she had doing the play. "She would tell me that she felt nauseous and ready to throw up, that's how scared she was."

The doctor created a fitting for the inside of Bette's mouth to help hold her teeth in place that would still allow her to speak and to perform without it being noticed, but she had to get used to it. "She had to wear an orthodontic appliance, and for most people it would have taken at least a week to get used to it," recalled Prince. "But Bette had tremendous agility with her lips and tongue, and she went back on stage with it as if it wasn't there."

However, dental issues were only a part of the problem. Bette felt the cast and crew had teamed up against her. She found the entire experience a very unhappy one and announced that she would exit the role after the fourth months of bookings were complete. Shelley Winters replaced her, and the play carried on for another five months.

Some 25 years later, during her final film, *Wicked Stepmother,* issues related to osteomyelitis and the state it had left her mouth in would drive her to once again exit a production. With Davis never returning to the production, the story behind the making and completion of the black comedy would become legendary ... certainly more so than the film itself.

The starlet Bette Davis.

Bette Davis early in her career.

2

"At first Bette insisted she was from 'the old school' and resisted any improvisation. But after a day or two, she came around to trying it my way, and actually seemed to enjoy it. Being extemporaneous was something new and challenging."

- Larry Cohen, Writer/Director of *Wicked Stepmother*

Chapter 2

Climb to Stardom

Bette Davis remarked in 1983, after undergoing a mastectomy, followed by a stroke, "I wouldn't want to live if I could never act again." *It was with this thought in mind that she exited* **Wicked Stepmother**, *hoping to never see the figure she saw in the dailies. On viewing the first week's footage she said, "People will be horrified at the footage on me."* *Whether she believed that medical treatment and rest would help restore her to a more youthful figure is unclear, but in interviews, after the story of her walking off the picture took shape, she told reporters, "I think that for the good of my future career I honestly had no choice."*

Unfortunately, there was no future career to protect.

...

Bette Davis once remarked, "Old age is no place for sissies." In fact, it was a quote embroidered onto a pillow that sat on the sofa in her living room.

By the time she had made that remark – and placed the pillow in her home – she had lived some 70 years and made nearly 80 films. She had lived long and hard. After a mastectomy and stroke at the age of 75, life and work both became more difficult. Having been in the limelight for six decades, it was hard to recede from the Hollywood spotlight.

"Bette might have been luckier if I hadn't seen her that night appearing as a presenter at the Golden Globes," recalled writer and director Larry Cohen. "If my heart hadn't gone out to the outrageous lady with partial facial paralysis who limped on to stage."

It was Cohen who envisioned a film starring Bette Davis as a stepmother wreaking havoc on her grown stepchildren in downtown Los Angeles. After some 102 films, TV movies, and television series appearances, the legend was out of work. Cohen felt that she would be more appreciative of work than a standing ovation or award for a lifetime of service to Hollywood – and what a lifetime of service it was. She indeed had come a long way.

Born on April 5, 1908, Ruth Elizabeth Davis was called Betty as a child. Growing up in the suburbs of Lowell, Massachusetts, she was the daughter of Harlow Morrell Davis - a patent attorney - and Ruth Augusta "Ruthie" Favór. Her younger sister, Barbara Harriet, known

43

as Bobby, was born in 1909. Their father was a patent attorney.

In 1915, after their parents separated, Betty and Bobby attended a boarding school in the Berkshires in western Massachusetts. Ruthie Davis had found work as a portrait photographer and moved her daughters to New York City. It was about this time that Betty changed the spelling of her name to "Bette" after reading the novel, *La Cousine Bette* by Honoré de Balzac.

Bette would return to Massachusetts where she attended Cushing Academy. It was there that she met her future husband, Harmon "Ham" Nelson, whom she would marry in 1932.

"The reason I wanted to go into theater was because of an actress named Peg Entwistle," Bette once recalled. She had seen Entwistle in a production of Henrik Ibsen's "The Wild Duck" in 1926 and decided she too wanted to be an actress. She would never get the opportunity to thank Entwistle for inspiring her career. In 1932, Entwistle would kill herself at the age of 24 by jumping from the "H" in the Hollywoodland sign.

Bette auditioned for Eva LeGallienne's Manhattan Civic Repertory but was rejected. After graduating from Cushing Academy, she enrolled in John Murray Anderson - Robert Milton School of Theatre and Dance, where Lucille

Ball was one of her classmates. She auditioned for George Cukor's stock theater company in Rochester, New York, and in 1929 she made her stage debut at Greenwich Village's Provincetown Playhouse production of "The Earth Between." Her first paid acting assignment was that of a chorus girl in the play "Broadway."

In 1929, Bette was then hired to play Hedwig, the character she had seen Peg Entwistle play in "The Wild Duck." The play took her on the road to Philadelphia, Washington, and Boston, before she returned to New York, making her formal Broadway debut at the age of 21 in "Broken Dishes."

A screen test for Universal Pictures followed in 1930 and landed her in Hollywood where she was assigned a small role in her first film, *The Bad Sister*, in 1931. After several additional small roles in forgettable movies like *Seed, Waterloo Bridge,* and *Way Back Home,* Universal dropped her contract. The studio did not see the makings of a star.

She considered going to back to New York and the theater, but Warner Bros. saw something in her and offered her work. She moved to Warner Bros. in 1932, and found success in the studio's production of *The Man Who Played God*. She would begin to thrive at Warner Bros., making 14 features over the next three years and becoming the studio's most promising commodity and respected leading lady.

Over the next 50-plus years, she would star in more than 100 films; be the first actress nominated for a ten Academy Awards; serve as the first female president of the Academy of Motion Picture Arts and Sciences; and the first woman to receive the American Film Institute's Lifetime Achievement Award.

By the latter part of the 1980s work had become scarce, and her career became one of appearances on talk shows; as a presenter on awards shows; and appearances as the honorary recipient for lifetime achievements like the Film Society of Lincoln Center Lifetime Achievement Award, the Legion of Honor from France, and Italy's Campione d'Italia.

Though she never won a Golden Globe for Best Actress, Bette agreed to make an appearance at the 1986 Golden Globe Awards to present the award for Best Picture. She had received Globe nominations for Best Actress three times - for *All About Eve, Pocketful of Miracles,* and *What Ever Happened to Baby Jane?.* However, it wasn't until 1974 that she walked off with an award when The Hollywood Foreign Press honored her with its prestigious Cecil B. DeMille Award.

In the audience that night in 1986 was a director named Larry Cohen. Seeing her warmly accept the applause and ovation from the crowd he was humbled by her lifetime of accomplishments and saddened by the fact that her greatest years were behind her. While she appeared grateful for the praise, recognition, and attention, he suspected that she would be even more grateful for an offer of work. So, he set out to craft a film with her in mind.

Bette Davis in *Jezebel*.

Bette Davis would be one of Warner Bros. biggest stars.

Initially directors were not sure how best to use her and she was blonde, brunette, homebody and vamp. She showed them she could do it all.

3

"*Why hadn't I just minded my own business and let her alone? She never asked for my help. Bette Davis never asked for anyone's help. That wasn't her style.*"

- Larry Cohen, Writer/Director of *Wicked Stepmother*

Chapter 3

Hanging on to Stardom

*I*n 1949, despite the less than spectacular performance of her last few films, Bette Davis renegotiated her contract with Warner Bros. to make four films for the studio and be paid $10,285 per week. It would make her the highest-paid woman in the United States. Though, much to her dismay, Jack Warner, head of the studio, refused to give her script approval. He had her cast in **Beyond the Forest**, a film that she made clear to him that she didn't want to make. Davis mustered her strength and begrudgingly completed the film. She then requested he release her from her contract. Jack Warner gladly obliged, thinking Davis was washed up. Davis proved him wrong when she landed the lead in **All About Eve** at 20th Century-Fox.*

...

On January 24, 1986, The Hollywood Foreign Press held its 43rd annual awards ceremony to honor the best of film and television for 1985. On hand to deliver the award for Best Picture was Bette Davis. Wearing a black dress with balloon sleeves and a purple-sequined torso, she donned her heavy reading glasses and labored through the list of nominees. After she read off the nominated films, including *Kiss of the Spider Woman, The Color Purple, Runaway Train* and *Witness,*

she played with the audience before announcing the winner by standing there in silence. She looked out over the crowd and said dryly, "I know, I'm just being mean." She looked out at the audience again after

opening the envelope, and failing to name the winner, she enjoyed having the full attention of the crowd. "But then, everybody knows I'm very mean anyway."

Davis seemed to delight in the suspense of her captive audience and paused a moment longer before announcing *Out of Africa* and presenting the award to director and producer Sydney Pollack. She then stood alongside Pollack, with her hands firmly placed on her hips, as he delivered his acceptance speech. She seemed uninterested in sharing the stage with anyone, as the attention moved away from her.

"Certainly it was a shocking sight to behold," recalled producer Larry Cohen, seeing Bette Davis at the Golden Globes that year, from his seat in the crowd. "But once Bette started to speak, she was unmistakably the brilliant queen of Warner Bros. As of that night, I was determined to create a project that would bring Bette back. And I wouldn't give up until she agreed to do it."

Larry Cohen had the opportunity to attend The Golden Globes that evening, but not because he had delivered a film in 1985. As both director and writer of *The Stuff*, Cohen's horror film would never receive the acclaim or admiration of the Hollywood Foreign Press. It wouldn't even afford him the chance to mix with the illustrious A-list power brokers of Hollywood. "I only got a ringside table at the Golden Globes because I showed up with my sister, Ronni Chasen, one of the industry's foremost publicists," recalled Cohen.

Dressed in a black tux and elbowing up alongside the Hollywood elite, Cohen was in his element, soaking up the sights and sounds and faces of people he had long-admired. He was loving it. He recalled that when Bette Davis was announced as presenter of the next award, "There was thunderous applause, which changed into waves of shock as she appeared on stage, dragging one withered leg behind her," Cohen said. "Bette couldn't have weighed more than 80 pounds, and she was clearly recovering from a stroke."

Even so, the sight of Bette Davis impressed and dazzled Cohen. "My motive was to do good for someone who'd given so many generations of moviegoers such continued enjoyment."

Larry Cohen had been raised on classic movies. Born on July 15, 1941, he was fascinated by the movies at an early age and was specifically attracted to Warner Bros. "It was a great studio–they had really ballsy movies and political movies ... They were shot at a fast pace with a lot of action and fast talk, as opposed to MGM movies, which were a lot slower and more luxurious."

Cohen started his career as a writer for television, working on shows like *Surfside 6, Checkmate, The Defenders, The Fugitive* and *Rat Patrol.* In 1966 he helped craft the sequel to the hit *The Magnificent Seven*, but the film, *Return of the Seven,* was a pale comparison to the original and was critiqued as "plodding" and "cliche-ridden."

His next film, starring Robert Goulet, *I Deal in Danger,* was a compilation of four episodes of a TV series he had written called *Blue Light*. Television seemed to provide more opportunities for the young writer, and he found himself busy with shows like *Custer, Coronet Blue* and *The Invaders*.

Cohen persevered with feature film work and by the 1970s, he was branching off into directing and producing his own films, like *Bone, Black Caesar,* and *Hell Up in Harlem.* His biggest success, *It's Alive,* was initially passed over when changes in management at Warner Bros. left the film with little promotion and a limited release in 1974. After a change in leadership again, Cohen convinced the studio to release the film again on a larger scale in 1977, and the film pulled in more than $7 million. It spawned several sequels like *It Lives Again* in 1978, and he would tackle other horrors like *Q-The Winged Serpent* in 1982 and *The Stuff* in 1985.

Little did Bette Davis know that her arrival in Hollywood, way back in 1930, would have such an impact on actors and filmmakers like Larry Cohen. Davis would later recount that no one from Universal was even there to meet her train when she arrived from New York, and she was disheartened. In reality a studio employee had actually been sent to greet her and waited patiently for her arrive, but the employee eventually left because, "I saw nobody who looked like an actress."

Her less than lustrous initial arrival in Hollywood was met with more dismay when chief of production at Universal Studios, Carl Laemmle, found her lacking in "star quality" and was thinking of canceling her contract. It was cinematographer Karl Freund who told him that she had "lovely eyes" and helped her land her first movie role in *Bad Sister* in 1931.

Laemmle was still unimpressed, suggesting Davis had "about as much sex appeal as Slim Summerville" - one of her gangly male co-stars. During her brief time at Universal, in addition to her films for the studio, she was loaned out to Columbia Pictures for *The Menace* and then Capital Films for *Hell's House*, but her performances made little impact, and she thought her movie career was over.

Planning to return to New York, she was shocked to learn that she was offered the leading lady role in Warner Bros.' film *The Man Who Played God* after actor George Arliss had suggested her for the part. The role would mark her breakthrough and she would forever be grateful to Arliss. Warner Bros. initially signed her to a five-year contract, but would extend it numerous times, keeping her grounded at the studio for the next 18 years.

Of Human Bondage in 1934 would be considered her first major dramatic performance and would earn her wide critical acclaim. While most of Hollywood's leading ladies avoided playing unsympathetic characters, Bette saw them as a chance to test her acting skills.

Davis hoped the strong part would encourage Jack Warner, head of the studio, to loan her to Columbia to star alongside Clark Gable in *It Happened One Night,* but Warner refused. The Oscar-winning part went to Claudette Colbert. It would be the first of a number of contentious encounters with Warner.

Bette landed her next substantive role in 1935 in *Dangerous.* The *New York Times* noted that she was quickly "becoming one of the most interesting of our screen actresses" and she earned her first Academy Award for Best Actress for her part as a down-and-out actress.

The Petrified Forest in 1936 had her co-starring alongside Leslie Howard and Humphrey Bogart and would be followed by a few forgettable pictures. Davis grew frustrated that Warner Bros. was wasting her in lackluster pictures. She challenged the studio by breaking her contract and left to work in the United Kingdom.

Warner Bros., filed suit against her and she appeared in court in Britain where barrister, Sir Patrick Hastings, who represented Warner Bros., called her "a naughty young lady" and asked the court to quickly resolve the situation. The British press didn't help the situation when Bette was portrayed as a spoiled Hollywood actress who was ungrateful for her success. She lost the case and returned to Hollywood to meet the terms of her contract. Though she had lost the case, she put Hollywood executives on notice and would give newfound power to other actors who began to challenge the status quo, creating cracks in the walls surrounding the longstanding Hollywood studio contract system.

Marked Woman, in 1937, cast her as a prostitute in the gangster drama. Several more forgettable features followed that year until 1938, when *Jezebel* cast her as a strong-minded southern belle alongside Henry Fonda. The role would earn her a second Academy Award.

Jezebel catapulted her into the most successful period of her career, and landed her on the annual Quigley Poll of the "Top Ten Money Making Stars" for the next several years. The poll was compiled by votes from movie exhibitors across the United States for stars that earned the highest revenue in theaters over the prior year. In addition to dollar earnings she would continue to earn acclaim with nominations for Best Actress for *Dark Victory* (1940), *The Letter* and *Little Foxes* (1941), *Now Voyager* (1943), and *Mr. Skeffington* (1945).

The six years between 1939 and 1945 would mark one of her most prolific periods, totaling some 20 feature films, including box office hits like *The Old Maid, Juarez, The Private Lives of Elizabeth and Essex, All This and Heaven Too,* and *The Man Who Came to Dinner.*

She had become Warner Bros.' most profitable star, and she was first in line for every major female role at the studio. One of Davis' strengths was her willingness to play parts in which the character might be older, less glamorous, or unsympathetic.

Davis was downright unlikable when she played Regina in *The Little Foxes* in 1941. It was roles like this that many of her counterparts, including Joan Crawford, Katherine Hepburn and Norma Shearer, avoided. While most of her contemporaries were less inclined to play a villain, she enjoyed the challenge.

In 1941 she took on an even more important role in the industry when she became the first female president of the Academy of Motion Picture Arts and Sciences. However, she quickly grew disillusioned with the post and resigned, feeling the committee wanted her only as a figurehead and wasn't interested in her ideas. She exited the leadership role after just two months.

Frustration continued when she starred opposite Miriam Hopkins in *Old Acquaintance* in 1943. The film pitted two old friends against each other when one of them becomes a successful novelist. The production was full of tension because Davis thought Hopkins was trying to upstage her. It would be one of the first on-set rivalries in which Davis clashed with her fellow female co-star.

In 1944, she played herself in the film *Hollywood Canteen* in support of the war effort. She would later say, "There are few accomplishments in my life that I am sincerely proud of. The Hollywood Canteen is one of them."

Her demands and troubling behavior on the set began to earn her a reputation for being too difficult to work with. During filming of *Mr. Skeffington,* she reportedly refused to film certain scenes for director Vincent Sherman. She also demanded that additional sets be built even though they were not needed. She crafted her own dialogue, rather than using what was written in the script. She frustrated her fellow actors, as well as the screenwriter.

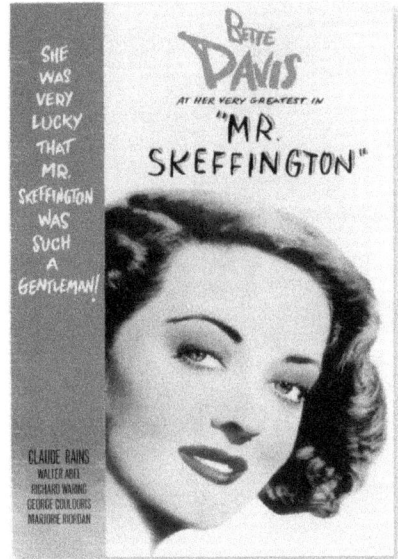

By the latter half of the 1940s, her career began to suffer. She refused to make *Mildred Pierce,* and the role instead went to Joan Crawford who walked away with the Best Actress Oscar for her performance. Bette had opted to make *The Corn in Green* instead, and the movie was a failure. Academy Award nominations disappeared and she wouldn't earn another nod until the 1950s. She made only five more pictures between 1946 and 1949. It wouldn't be until 1950 when she took on the role of Margo Channing in *All About Eve* that she would be back at the top of pack, but her stay was short-lived and the 1950s would prove a difficult time for the star.

Celeste Holme, Bette Davis, and Hugh Marlowe in 'All About Eve.'

4

"She hadn't made a theatrical feature in over 10 years, and her career had been relegated to parts in television movies."

- Larry Cohen, Writer/Director of *Wicked Stepmother*

Chapter 4

The Lean Years

Bette Davis was not Twentieth Century-Fox's first choice for **All About Eve**. In fact, she wasn't the second, third or even the fourth choice. The first actress originally considered to play Margo Channing was Susan Hayward. Director Joseph Mankiewicz felt that Hayward was perfect, but producer Darryl Zanuck said that she was "too young," and rejected the casting. Others cast aside were Marlene Dietrich, who Zanuck felt was "too German," and Gertrude Lawrence, who wanted the script rewritten so that she could sing a torch song. While Zanuck wanted Barbara Stanwyck, she was not available. Other leading ladies, including Tallulah Bankhead, Ingrid Bergman, and Joan Crawford were considered before Claudette Colbert ultimately accepted the part. However, shortly before filming Colbert dropped out due to an injury and Mankiewicz turned to Bette Davis as a last resort. Bette, rebounding from the end of an 18-year association with Warner Bros., gladly accepted the part, calling it, "one of the best I'd ever read."

...

In 1988 Bette Davis was 80 years old. After having viewed the rushes of her work on *Wicked Stepmother*, she recoiled at the image of a frail, emaciated, old woman in a frightful red wig. A stroke and a bout with cancer in the mid 1980s - combined with her addiction to smoking - made it nearly impossible for her to put on weight. She appeared rail thin even though the camera would add pounds to her appearance.

To add insult to injury, effects from a broken hip she suffered, three months after her stroke, never quite healed and made her physical movements awkward on camera. The icing on the cake came from her stilted speech as she struggled to deliver her lines while keeping her dentures in place. While Davis was known for her iconic speech patterns, she was now becoming a caricature of herself.

The only parts of her that remained in tact were her iconic eyes - and the cigarette that was constantly poised between her fingers or her lips. The eyes launched the number one song on the *Billboard* pop charts in 1981, and the cigarette had become a prop that was never far away. While the legend known as Bette Davis was forming as far back as her early years of stardom, it was the acting that drove her. From *Jezebel, Dark Victory, The Letter,* and *The Little Foxes* she became one the most formidable of actresses working in Hollywood. Her sarcastic wit, rolling eyes and cigarette prop would become part of pop culture after her portrayal of Margo Channing in 1950's *All About Eve*. They were still there, but the rest was fading away.

All About Eve, like *Wicked Stepmother*, came at the most welcome of times and showed Davis still could command attention if the part and the script were right. She had appeared less onscreen over the previous few years and had focused on family

life. In 1945, she married artist William Grant Sherry. She was drawn to him because he was a Hollywood outsider who claimed that even he never knew who she was. It was her third marriage, after previous marriages to Ham Nelson and Arthur Farnsworth. She took time off in 1947 to have her daughter, Barbara Davis Sherry. At the time, she considered completely retiring from acting, to focus on motherhood, but it was not to be.

The marriage was volatile to say the least. The two argued often, but they would make up when Bette calmed down. She berated him for not making any money and forcing her to be the full-time breadwinner. However, he refused to take her abuse. "She had to dominate her men, and when they wouldn't let her, she didn't like it," he once remarked.

She claimed that during one heated argument, he rose from his chair; he walked across the room; picked up a small oak table; and turned it over on top of her. He walked out of the room and left her to pick herself up off the floor and clean up the mess.

Marion Richards, a young woman Bette had hired as her daughter B.D.'s governess, saw the marital woes up close. She said whenever Bette and William were together they argued. "She was always on his case, calling him a prince, saying she was making all the money. Then he'd offer to go to work, and she'd say no, because she'd have to pay more taxes. He was damned if he did, damned if he didn't."

Though Bette was the breadwinner, she was not in much demand; and in her frustration, she lashed out at those nearby. Film offers were not as strong as they once had been. Even so, Bette signed a new contract with Warner Bros. in January 1949 that would make her the highest-paid woman in the United States. Jack Warner's refusal to give Bette script approval left her unhappy. She continued to lash out.

She had made the comedy *June Bride* only to suffer at the hands of the critics. While the film didn't perform terribly at the box office, Bette had never been comfortable with comedy, and it showed onscreen. A film critic for *The New Yorker* commented, "She conducts herself throughout the film with the grim competent air of a prison warden."

June Bride, Beyond the Forest, and *Winter Meeting* were all films that she would have rather avoided, but was forced to make. Unhappy at work, she carried her anger home and continued to argue with Sherry until the two were barely speaking. She walked out on him and filed for divorce in October 1949 but by then she'd found someone new.

Estranged from Sherry, and unhappy with work in Hollywood, Bette was at one of the lowest points of her life. She reconciled briefly with Sherry, but the marriage was doomed. She took work in the film *Payment on Demand*, but a gossip columnist hinted that she was having an affair with her married co-star, Barry Sullivan. While Sullivan denied the affair, the rumors created tension between Davis and Sherry. On the last day of filming, Sherry arrived on the set, demanding that she go home with him. He confronted Sullivan about his relationship with his wife. Police were soon called, and her husband was kicked off the set. Soon after, Bette reinstated the divorce proceedings.

It was during this low point that producer Darryl F. Zanuck reluctantly offered Bette the role of an aging theater actress named Margo Channing. *All About Eve*, released in 1950, would mark the only real standout film Bette would make for the next decade.

Davis called the script the best she'd read and accepted it immediately. Filming went smoothly, though tension with costar Celeste Holm was reported. Critics and fans responded favorably to the film and made it a hit at the box office. Bette was once again nominated for an Academy Award. She also won a Best Actress award from the Cannes Film Festival, as well as honors from the New York Film Critics Circle Award and the San Francisco Film Critics Circle. She wanted to be the first actress to be awarded three Best Actress Oscars, but was grateful for the acclaim and the work, even though she lost the honor to Judy Holliday for *Born Yesterday*.

Aside from the success of the film, another happy development occurred during filming when she fell for her leading man, Gary Merrill. As divorce proceedings were moving forward with her current marriage, she looked to remarry with Merrill; however, he also needed to finalize a divorce from his current wife before the two could wed. Bette's divorce from Sherry had been finalized a few weeks earlier on July 3. In Mexico, on July 28, 1950, Merrill finalized his divorce from Barbara Leeds. Bette and Gary would wed that same day. Sherry also gave his consent to allow Merrill to adopt his and Bette's daughter B.D..

The Merrill union would carry Bette through the 1950s, and she would attempt to settle down into a stable marriage and family. After completing B.D.'s adoption by Merrill, the couple adopted two other children, Margot and Michael. They would also work alongside each other, appearing onscreen in *Another Man's Poison* in 1951 and *Phone Call From a Stranger* in 1952.

As the 1950s progressed, film offers declined for Bette. Whether it was the idea that she could be difficult to work with, or the fact that she was now an aging actress - and Hollywood was more interested in the likes of Marilyn Monroe, Susan Hayward, and Grace Kelly - it was a tough for her to handle. *The Star* (1952), *The Virgin Queen* (1955), *The Catered Affair* (1956) and *Storm Center* (1956), represented the only chances that fans had to see Davis on the big screen during the first half of the decade.

When film work became scarce, Bette accepted offers from television. While most actresses avoided the new medium, her desire to work had her making guest appearances in programs like *The 20th Century-Fox Hour, Schlitz Playhouse, The Ford Television Theater, Studio 57, General Electric Theater, Alfred Hitchcock Presents*, and other weekly series work. She did find film work with two supporting roles in 1959 in *John Paul Jones* and *Scapegoat,* but it wouldn't be until 1961 that she would land a major part in a film.

Bette would work also with husband Gary Merrill in 1959 in a stage show called "An Evening With Carl Sandburg." By then, the marriage was on the rocks and the two would go through a bitter divorce in 1960.

Producer William Frye said Bette's volatile outbursts were one of the main strains on the marriage. He claimed many of her Hollywood friends became reluctant to socialize with her due to her outbursts. "She was capable of blowing up at any moment, and no host or hostess wanted to risk a fierce outburst in the middle of a delicately constructed social affair."

Frye recalled during the Merrill marriage that he worked with Bette on a TV project called *Fraction of a Second* for a series called *Suspicion*. Even though it was TV, the two had thought that the project was a good one. "Bette said she was keen to do it, and the rehearsals went well. I knew it was going to be a good film. With Bette, however, just when you thought everything was shaping up nicely, all hell would break loose."

Frye said that just as filming was about to begin, things took a turn for the worse. "At five a.m., the day shooting was to start, [and] my phone rang. 'Bill, it's Bette. You're going to have to get somebody else for the part. There's no way I can do the picture.'"

Frye replied, "Bette, you're due at the studio in an hour for makeup. You have to do this picture."

"Well, I won't be there. I'm not feeling well. I'm sick," she told him.

"Have you called a doctor?" he asked.

"No. I don't need a doctor. I just can't do it. You'll have to get somebody else," was all she said.

After a long silence, Frye said, "Bette, I'm going to tell you something, and I want you to listen. [*Fraction of a Second*] was written especially for you. Besides, you need to work. You need the money. And if you don't do it, the studio will sue you so fast that you'll never work again. Now, I'm going to send Dr. Bethea to see you. William Bethea is a friend of mine who lives near you. We'll revise the shooting schedule so we can shoot around you today."

Frye said that later that morning he received a call from the doctor, who reported that the star wasn't sick at all. She and Merrill had had a fight the night before that had started inside the house but got wilder and moved outside. At some point during the altercation, Bette fell - or was pushed, as Frye recalled - onto a gravel driveway. One side of her face was badly bruised and scratched; so, she couldn't be in front of the cameras. Bette did finally complete the project in 1958.

After the marriage ended, Davis and Merrill would go their separate ways, but time seemed to heal old wounds. Years later, when Bette's daughter B.D. released a nasty tell-all book about her mother in 1985, Merrill appeared at a Hollywood bookstore with a sign telling readers not to buy the lies in *My Mother's Keeper*. Though Bette hadn't spoken to Merrill in some 15 years she was surprised by his thoughtful actions and sent him a thank you note for standing up for her.

In an interview around the time of Bette's death and the video release of her final film, *Wicked Stepmother*, Merrill recalled, "When I think of my marriage to Bette, I think we were playing at it the way we played roles in the movies ... We fell in love in the movies. Subconsciously, we just went on after the movie was finished. As the demands of real life set in, we realized the premise was wrong."

With the marriage to Merrill over, Bette really had only one place to seek solace - and that was work. But would Hollywood have her? An opportunity from an unlikely source would prove that even if industry bigwigs had doubts, fans would still turn out to see Bette Davis.

5

"My motive was to do good for someone who'd given so many generations of moviegoers such continued enjoyment. Instead, I made it impossible for her to ever work again."

- Larry Cohen, Writer/Director of *Wicked Stepmother*

Chapter 5

The Wicked Jane Hudson

Whatever was to become of **Wicked Stepmother** after Bette Davis' departure had yet to be determined, but for Larry Cohen the facts were simple - it was her name and face that inspired the film in the first place. Fortunately, Cohen's Larco Productions shelled out a hefty fee to insure its aging star; and after her exit, the move would prove to be a shrewd one. The funds would come in handy in keeping the production afloat during the star's absence as he reworked the picture without her.

A million-dollar insurance policy enabled Cohen to keep his production going until actress Barbara Carrera arrived to take on the character that she originally was contracted to play, but in a new and expanded role. While Carrera wouldn't act alongside the leading lady, Cohen would look for an inventive way to explain Davis' absence as he retooled the script to complete his film. This tact would pit him *against his star when she learned that the movie would include her after all.*

For Davis, it was a reminder of battles from days gone by. She'd been up against some of the best directors, producers, actors and actresses who tried her patience and tested her fortitude, but in the end she outlasted them all. Her work in the 1962 classic **What Ever Happened to Baby Jane?** *would test her on every level, but the iconic film would set Bette on a direct course that would ultimately lead to the concept for* **Wicked Stepmother**.

...

In many ways, the success of *What Ever Happened to Baby Jane?* propelled Bette Davis through the 60s and 70s, and the film became an iconic piece of cinematic history. The film and Bette's role in it were in large part the inspiration for Larry Cohen's desire to build his *Wicked Stepmother* around her. It was the sheer force of Davis' performance, and the success of the film, that not only ensured her work for years to come, but also launched a cottage industry of aging actresses thrust into danger in hopes of reaping profits at the box office. Producer of the TV series *Thriller,* William Frye, told *Vanity Fair* that it was he who had "found a terrific book by Henry Farrell called *What Ever Happened to Baby Jane?*"

Frye recalled that after reading it several times, "I decided that, while it was too long and complex for *Thriller*, it could work beautifully as a feature film—specifically, my first feature film."

Frye had been a longtime producer in radio and TV who longed to step up to feature films and hoped that a strong story might land him there. "I gave the book to Bette, and she loved it," he said. "I also gave a copy to Olivia de Havilland, whom I thought would be right to play the bedridden sister. Ida Lupino, who had directed many *Thriller* episodes for me, was my choice to direct."

Frye shared his idea with Universal executive Lew Wasserman, but Wasserman passed on the idea. Bette had recently made a guest appearance on the Universal series *Wagon Train*, and Wasserman didn't think she was very good. A few months later, director Robert Aldrich acquired the rights to the book. Frye said he had heard from Ida Lupino that Aldrich wanted Joan Crawford to star in *Baby Jane.*

One story suggests that it was Crawford who'd actually given the book to Aldrich and approached him to direct her, after having worked with him several years earlier. It was her urging that convinced Aldrich to purchase the film rights. She in turn had her sights set on her co-star - Bette Davis.

While Crawford and Davis were well aware of each other as two of the leading actresses in Hollywood of the 1940s, they were in many ways rivals whose paths rarely crossed professionally or personally. Davis' disdain for Crawford was fairly well known among the Hollywood set. She always felt that Crawford was more of a star than an actress, while she saw herself as an actress rather than a star. Davis' insecurities over Crawford's successful career, popularity at both MGM and Warner Bros. and her success with men, as well, may have helped intensify her dislike of a woman she really never knew.

Crawford, on the other hand, never uttered a negative word about Davis as an actress, a star, or a woman. In fact, she longed to work with her and admired her talent.

Crawford and Davis had met before. Back in the fall of 1945 when Crawford was starring in *Mildred Pierce* and Davis in *The Corn is Green*, the two women crossed paths at the Warner Bros. commissary during lunch. While Crawford's film would be the hit of the year, Davis' more expensive picture failed miserably. At lunch that afternoon Crawford walked up to Davis during lunch to invite her to a dinner party. While Joan stood there, Bette kept eating and barely looked up, and never invited Joan to sit down. She then refused her invitation.

However, to Bette's credit, after Crawford won her Oscar a few months later, becoming only the second Best Actress award-winner at Warner Bros. - Bette Davis was the first - Bette sent Joan a telegram. It simply said, "Congratulations."

Ironically, had Bette not turned down the lead in *Mildred Pierce* she likely would have won that third Oscar she so coveted.

Now, years later, in January 1962, glittering and dressed to the nines, Joan Crawford nervously walked backstage at the Royale Theatre on Broadway. She was there to see Bette Davis. Accompanied by writer Chuck Bowden and actress Paula Laurence, Crawford had some arm support for an encounter about which she was apprehensive. Davis was playing the supporting role of Maxine Faulk in *The Night of the Iguana* in 1961. It was much needed work for Bette, who hadn't had a strong film role or much else for some time and the income and acting work were indeed welcome. However, the play itself was an unhappy experience for the veteran actress. She was starring in a secondary role to Margaret Leighton's leading one. Leighton would subsequently win a Tony award for her performance. The play would be named the best American play of 1961-62 by the Outer Critic's Circle, and most of the praise and attention was directed at the star rather than the supporting performers. Davis was furious when Leighton received standing ovations and rave reviews while Davis went overlooked in the secondary role.

Joan Crawford was about to change Davis' life with the offer of a film role. It couldn't have come from a more unlikely source and Davis almost ruined the chance. As the quick and somewhat unnecessary introductions were made - without any real or false show business embraces - Davis got right to the point. "Let's make this quick, Joan," said Davis. "I'm going to the country in five minutes."

Weeks later, Bette Davis herself had lunch with William Frye in New York and told him, "You'll never believe it," she said, "but Crawford gave me a copy of the book with a note suggesting I play the sister. I told her never. I know the book, and the only part I'm interested in is Baby Jane."

Davis said that Crawford told her, "I've always wanted to work with you," ... and that she had ... "at last found the perfect picture for us to work together."

"Together?" Bette reportedly questioned, suggesting Crawford was, "full of shit."

Crawford then gave her a copy of the book and told her about the story and the potential film. Davis, already aware of the story, reportedly went into hysterics, ranting about how she had wanted to buy the property herself, but that she couldn't stand the idea of having to work with Crawford in a movie version of it. She was suspicious of the enterprise and said to those present, "If she thinks I'm going to play that stupid bitch in the wheelchair, she's got another thing coming!"

Davis also found out from Crawford that the film rights belonged to Robert Aldrich, a director with whom Crawford had worked in a drama called *Autumn Leaves*

(1955). Crawford reportedly had a brief affair with the director but the two remained friendly and in contact, with Crawford often asking him when they would work together again. She had also once supposedly asked him to help her find a picture to co-star her and Davis.

Aldrich was a seasoned director who started his career back in 1941. He left college for a minor job at the RKO Radio Pictures and quickly became involved in film production as an assistant director, working with filmmakers like Jean Renoir, Abraham Polonsky, and Charlie Chaplin as he developed his craft. His early success as a director came in television in the early 1950s. He directed his first feature film, *The Big Leaguer,* in 1953. He followed it with features like *Vera Cruz* and *Apache* (1954), *Kiss Me Deadly* and *The Big Knife* (1955), *Attack* (1956), and *Ten Seconds to Hell* (1959), among others.

Aldrich read Henry Farrell's book, *What Ever Happened to Baby Jane?* after it was published in 1960 and had his agent, William Morris, buy the film rights in July 1961. Aldrich was at work filming *Sodom and Gomorrah;* so, he hired Lukas Heller, who was a relative newcomer with mostly a handful of TV projects to his name, to craft the screenplay. He sent Crawford a copy of the script in October 1961. A week later Crawford called him and simply said, "When do we start?"

With the script complete and Crawford on board, it was now time to get Davis signed to the picture. Walter Blake, an associate producer who had worked with Aldrich on the film *Attack* and was planning on producing *Baby Jane,* knew Davis from her years at Warner Bros. He was asked to meet with her following Crawford's initial offer and to get her to sign. He approached her with $25,000. "We knew she needed money," recalled Blake. "So we figured if we got her to sign the back of the check, legally she'd have to do it."

Blake called Davis at The Plaza Hotel in New York where she was staying during the run of *The Night of the Iguana.*

"Walter who? Never heard of you," she replied after answering his call.

"I knew you at Warner Bros., Miss Davis."

"Oh, yeah. What do you want?" she said coldly.

He was invited up to her suite where she greeted him wearing a simple pair of slacks, a blouse, hair tied back, little make-up, and smoking her usual cigarette. He offered her the script.

"I know about this," she replied. "Who's gonna direct?"

"Robert Aldrich," said Blake.

"Who the hell is he?" she snapped.

"He's directed nine films ... *Apache, Autumn Leaves, The Angry Hills* ..."

"Never heard of him. I bet he stinks," she responded. "Who's producing?"

"I am," said Blake.

"I bet you stink too," she offered.

Blake thought he'd failed at convincing her but left her the script and receded from the hotel to lick his wounds and regroup. Much to his surprise, Davis called him a short time later after having a chance to review the script. Davis reportedly hoped the studio might convince Alfred Hitchcock to direct the picture, but he was busy at Universal working on *The Birds* and *Marnie*.

"I read the thing," she said. "I'll be playing Jane, right?"

"Of course," he replied.

"Who's the other broad?" she asked, suspecting all along it was Crawford.

"We don't know yet," Blake lied.

Blake knew it would be trouble if Davis found out they already had inked a deal with Crawford and felt that the best way to play it was close to the vest and get her to sign the check he had before telling her who her co-star would be.

"I have a check with me for $25,000, Miss Davis. And I can give it to you if you'll sign on the back that you'll do the movie."

"What - $25,000 for a movie?" she bellowed.

"It's just a down payment," he assured her. "It's a binder to say that you'll do the movie. We can negotiate your salary, and what you'll get up front, all of that."

Davis signed the check that day and flew to Hollywood a day later to meet the director and work out the details of her contract.

When Bette Davis walked into her first production meeting to meet the director, sitting next to him was none other than Joan Crawford. Davis took one look and reportedly turned and walked out.

She looked at Blake with betrayal. "You've got to be kidding?" she said. "I won't work with her!"

"Well, Bette," said Blake. "You've got to. We just paid you $25,000.

Davis had been had. She knew it. She walked back into the room, sat down without so much as a hello or nod to Crawford, and got down to business.

When it came to contracts, both women worked out the details of their deals separately, with Davis expecting the star salary above her co-star, but it was Crawford who ultimately had the last laugh.

Davis signed on at a salary of $60,000, which included the $25,000 she had already received, along with 10 percent of the worldwide gross and $600 a week in living expenses. Crawford, on the other hand, opted to accept only $30,000 in salary in exchange for 15 percent of the gross and $1,500 a week in living expenses.

When the film became a smash in the U.S., Crawford would earn more than $600,000 to Davis' $400,000. As the film went into worldwide release, Crawford's profits outpaced Davis' take. Crawford reportedly earned more than $1 million from the film to Davis' $600,000, when box office totals eventually carried the film above $9 million.

But first, they had to get through the filming.

Few studios were interested in taking on financing of the film. As Jack Warner put it "I wouldn't give you one dime for those two washed-up old bitches."

However, Seven Arts, a smaller production house, agreed to finance the film, provided that the budget was kept under a million dollars. The feature would come in at $980,000 and would take just 36 days to shoot. Warner Bros. agreed to distribute the film.

In addition to Crawford and Davis as Blanche and Jane Hudson, Victor Buono took on a key supporting role which would earn him an Academy Award nomination. Other cast members included Maidie Norman, Anna Lee,

Marjorie Bennett and a young B.D. Merrill - Bette Davis's daughter - who played a neighbor of the Hudson sisters.

The story centers on two Hollywood sisters who live in an old, dilapidated house in Hollywood after their careers have passed them by. Jane, a one-time child star, has deteriorated into a caricature of her former self and isn't quite running on all cylinders. Blanche was an acclaimed actress, but is now confined to a wheelchair after a terrible car crash that left her paralyzed from the waist down.

The two sisters are dependent on one another - Jane for Blanche's financial savings and Blanche for Jane's services as caregiver. Underlying the relationship is the car crash in which Jane supposedly tried to kill Blanche one evening after drinking too much. The women unravel as Jane loses grip on reality and Blanche fights for her own survival, though dependent on Jane for everything.

The film features several key dramatic scenes for both actresses including one knock down fight scene where Jane kicks and beats poor Blanche after catching her trying to use the telephone to call for help. In the weighty scene Crawford refused to lay on the floor for fear that Davis would actually kick her; so, a dummy was brought in for Davis to pummel. Crawford was struck by how violently Davis attacked the dummy and was glad she that hadn't taken the chance. She then filmed her close ups on the floor separately.

While Davis and Crawford were in nearly every scene, the feature included strong performances from its notable co-stars. Maidie Norman appeared as housekeeper Elvira Stitt and Victor Bueno as Edwin Flagg. Norman had worked with Crawford nearly a decade earlier in *Torch Song*. Bueno was a relative newcomer, having worked mostly in television, but would return to work with Davis again in *Hush ... Hush, Sweet Charlotte*. Marjorie Bennett, Anna Lee, Wesley Addy were seasoned actors hired to fill out the cast.

In another key scene Jane is expected to lift Blanche from the bed to a wheelchair. Davis claimed that Crawford tied weights to herself to make herself heavier than normal that resulted in back injury for Davis. Crawford disputed this, but one story suggested Davis told her not to be a dead weight, because she had a bad back, and Crawford may have used the moment to make her co-star suffer. When Bette lifted Joan, Bette reportedly recoiled in pain and ended up in the hospital for a few days.

For years, rumors of the fighting and bad behavior on the set continued, but many who were on the set claimed that both actresses were actually quite professional with one another. Even though it was clear that the two women never got along and Davis often spoke poorly of Crawford, neither let the dislike of one another prevent them from getting their work done. Both needed the picture to succeed too badly to let personalities get in the way of their careers.

Bette in later years claimed that there was no feud. She went on to add that, "Like, dislike - these were not words I applied to Miss Crawford. Until we were cast as co-stars of *What Ever Happened to Baby Jane?*, I knew her only slightly. Even though for three years we had adjoining dressing rooms at Warners."

After the filming of *Baby Jane*, Davis admitted, "In truth, I did not know her any better after the film was completed."

The closest she came to offering a real opinion about Crawford was in her last autobiography when she wrote, "Joan was a pro. She was always punctual, always knew her lines. I will always thank her for giving me the opportunity to play the part of 'Baby Jane' Hudson."

In fact, the actresses caught reporters off guard during the filming of the movie when they were overheard having a conversation on the set, and the women played it up for the press.

"Of course, you know Joan, that everybody is trying to work up a feud between us."

"I know dear, isn't that ridiculous? We're much too professional for that," responded Crawford.

"Exactly, who has time for such silliness? We're much too busy making the picture."

"Of course," agreed Joan.

"You know what the word is around New York? The situation is so bad that your dressing room is at one end of the stage, and mine is at the other end. Now I ask you, look at those dressing rooms!" said Davis directing Crawford to their trailers that were about 20 feet apart.

"You know the only reason I am over there is I like to be near the cooling machine," said Crawford who always requested the set be cold.

"Oh no! I adore the cold," said Bette. "I'm liable to move over there with you."

"And we'll end the picture with our rooms side by side, fooling everyone," laughed Joan.

"I'll tell you one thing I hope this picture does. I hope it brings back women's pictures. The men have had it to themselves for far too long," said Davis. "But I must admit we had it pretty good for 15 years back there."

"We sure did," added Crawford. "But now everything is war and destruction on the screen."

According to several reports the women only had one major confrontation, and it came at the end of filming.

During one key bedroom scene, Crawford said she wasn't feeling well and asked Aldrich if they could take a break from filming. He agreed, but an agitated Davis complained, "You'd think after all these years we'd all be troupers." Crawford shot her a nasty look and stormed off the set. Filming completed on September 12, 1962.

The feature was pulled together and previewed quickly, only about 30-days later. Before opening, previews went over well and everyone at Warner Bros. and Seven Arts knew they had a blockbuster on their hands. The film held its premiere on October 26, 1962 in New York and opened across the country on October 31. Davis agreed to attend openings at theaters across New York City, even giving away Baby Jane dolls on stage, while Crawford and Davis both attended a press party at 21, a New York hot spot, to help promote the picture even further. The women spoke to reporters, but did so separately at opposite ends of the room to avoid interacting with one another.

The film was an immediate success when released in October 1962. Within 11 days, it reportedly covered the bulk of its production costs, eventually earning some $4 million in U.S. box office receipts and an additional $5 million in worldwide revenues. Davis would report that the film would eventually earn $10 million. The reviews were good, but not everyone gushed at the casting combination.

In his review in *The New York Times*, Bosley Crowther observed, "[Davis and Crawford] do get off some amusing and eventually blood-chilling displays of screaming sororal hatred and general monstrousness ... The feeble attempts that Mr. Aldrich has made to suggest the irony of two, once idolized and wealthy females living in such depravity, and the pathos of their deep-seated envy having brought them to this, wash out very quickly under the flood of sheer grotesquerie."

Variety wrote of the film, "Although the results heavily favor Davis (and she earns the credit), it should be recognized that the plot, of necessity, allows her to run unfettered through all the stages of oncoming insanity ... Crawford gives a quiet, remarkably fine interpretation of the crippled Blanche, held in emotionally by the nature and temperament of the role. Paul Beckley of the *New York Herald* wrote, "If Miss Davis' portrait of an outrageous slattern with the mind of an infant has something of the force of a hurricane, Miss Crawford's could be described at the eye of that hurricane, abnormally quiet, perhaps, but ominous and desperate."

Of their performances, Davis was considered over-the-top, but some took notice of Crawford's understated role.

Both actresses were thrilled to have a hit on their hands and Bette was further honored when she received an Academy Award nomination as best actress for her performance. Davis claimed until her death that Crawford didn't want her to win the award and actively campaigned against her. However, others suggest that Crawford was far too wise for that knowing that an Oscar win would only add to her 15 percent of the film's profits.

Crawford, however, did offer to accept the Best Actress Award at the 1963 ceremony for any actress who was not in attendance and won. When Anne Bancroft won the award for *The Miracle Worker* instead of Davis, she reportedly breezed by Bette, who was also standing backstage, without so much as a kind word. Crawford accepted the Oscar as if she were receiving it herself. Bette Davis always felt Crawford prevented her from winning the award, but many dispute this notion and think that Davis needed someone to blame for losing her third Academy Award.

The film did earn an Academy Award for Norma Koch for Best Costume Design. Both Crawford and Davis were nominated in the Best Actress category for BAFTA awards, the British equivalent of the Oscars - for their performances, but neither took home the award.

The success of the film would result in both Crawford and Davis being sought after for any number of horror films throughout the 60s, and into the 1970s. Actually, it was the horror film genre that garnered both actresses the most attention and money as the years passed, even though they both tried their hands at more serious fare.

Larry Cohen, by the 1980s had seen all the of Bette's horror films and knew that audiences still recalled her campy performances in *What Ever Happened to Baby Jane?*, *Dead Ringer*, *The Nanny*, and others. It was this very fact that convinced him that *Wicked Stepmother* could capitalize on Bette Davis' iconic status as the queen of Grand Guignol

to make his film - if he could land her as his star and find a studio to fund it. He even had an idea of how to capitalize on the history of Crawford and Davis in *Baby Jane* by getting Crawford into the film - even though she had been dead for more than a decade. However, knowing Davis had little nice to say of Crawford, Cohen failed to include the Crawford reference in the original shooting script.

6

"Bette Davis never asked for anyone's help. That wasn't her style."

- Larry Cohen, Writer/Director of *Wicked Stepmother*

Chapter 6

The Villainess Reigns

H ad **Wicked Stepmother** been completed with the star for whom it was originally intended for, it would have been quite a different film; however, like many Hollywood stories, movies often start off with the best of intentions and their paths from page to screen can take many twists and turns along way.

Another Bette Davis film, **Dead Ringer,** also turned out quite differently than originally intended. In that case, the story had first been made into a film back in 1946, as an inexpensive Mexican feature and Hollywood got the idea for an updated version 17 years later, as legendary leading ladies like Joan Crawford and Bette Davis found film work in horror films that raked in dollars if made on a lower-end budget.

The intended star, Lana Turner, would avoid the genre until the late 1960s, but had ventured into the world as murderess, most recently in **Portrait in Black**. However, Lana wanted to avoid being cast as a killer and villain where *possible. While her films often had the draw of murder and suspicion, Lana was more willing to be a victim, suspect or an unwilling participant rather than a cold-blooded killer. She turned down a dual role, leaving Warner Bros. to look elsewhere for their star of **Dead Ringer.** Bette Davis had no trouble being a murderess. She had been there before.*

...

"It began as an effort to help her resurrect her dormant career and ended with the final nail in the coffin of a legend." recalled *Wicked Stepmother* director Larry Cohen. "I never meant Bette Davis any harm. Just the opposite."

For her 80th birthday Bette said she didn't want a lot of fanfare. She told her personal assistant Kathryn Sermak that what she really wanted was, "one great role." Bette was aware of Cohen's project, but was not convinced the script was any good, but with the scripts few and far between, it was the only offer on the table.

Cohen himself had reservations about the aging star's health. Frail and limping after undergoing a mastectomy in 1983, she suffered several

strokes less than two week later. During her recovery, she then took a fall and broken her hip. Her health continued to be a concern. Her weight hovered around 90 pounds and Cohen knew that he would have trouble insuring the completion of the picture, but he believed her talent, her wit, and her personality were intact.

Bette never doubted her own ability and quitting a film was not like her - even when the script was inferior. This time she had convinced herself that the script had enough laughs, special effects, and shocks to succeed if she was the star.

With her frail appearance she would need every bit of help in the makeup and costume department to make her look her best. While Bette had never been overly concerned about looking like a glamour queen onscreen, she was vain enough to want to do as much as possible with what she had. When asked if she watched the rushes of her work, she admitted that she wanted to see the dailies of her work as she aged. "Sometimes on a picture, I do, especially lately on these television things - I have to look presentable. I want to know how I'm being photographed."

In her early years, she easily gussied herself up, but by her middle age, it had become more work. When she returned to the throws of work in the early 1960s the challenges began to present themselves.

With *What Ever Happened to Baby Jane?* and *Hush ...
Hush, Sweet Charlotte,* her characters were oddballs and the
screen required little in the way of glamour, but later it
would become more complicated. It was back around 1963
that she began to realize that her looks required more
attention to detail than they had before, if she were to
retain her movie queen status. It was the year that she
stepped into duel roles as twin sisters for *Dead Ringer* that
the challenge presented itself in a unique way.

The film originally started off as a horror called *Who
is Buried in My Grave?*, but was retitled by the time it was
released in 1964. Bette starred as twin sisters caught up in a

Mirror, mirror on the wall, now who's the fairest twin of all?

BETTE DAVIS & *BETTE DAVIS* & KARL MALDEN & PETER LAWFORD
DEAD RINGER.......For "Baby Jane" people!

WARNER BROS.

betrayal that tears them apart and a murder that brings them together. The story had been made into film back in 1946, as an inexpensive Mexican feature called *La Otra,* aka *Dead Pigeon*, with Dolores del Rio as the star. However, Warner Bros. got the idea for an updated version after Bette and Joan Crawford found themselves with a hit in *What Ever Happened to Baby Jane?* that raked in dollars and was produced on a low-end budget.

Jack Warner had acquired the script of "Who is Buried in My Grave?" intended for Lana Turner. He thought that it would spell big box office if it reminded fans of Turner's real-life scandal surrounding sex and murder in Hollywood, but Turner turned down the part, hoping to avoid being cast as a killer. Turner's lover, Johnny Stompanato, had been stabbed to death in the bedroom of her Beverly Hills home in 1958 by Turner's teenage daughter. The scandal had all of Hollywood talking and the story made headlines around the world. Lana weathered the storm but wanted to avoid being cast as a murderess.

After Turner had decided that the film wasn't right for her, Jack Warner quickly thought it might make a good vehicle for Davis. At one time, Davis had been Warner Bros. biggest leading lady, but she and Warner had a rocky relationship. Both had mellowed over the years and the success of *What Ever Happened to Baby Jane?* left Warner realizing Bette Davis' career still had some life left in it. Retitled *Dead Ringer*, the concept was similar enough in theme to *Baby Jane* to capitalize on the actress' recent successes. In some international markets, a title more similar to *What Ever Happened to Baby Jane?* was used when the film was released as *Who is Buried in My Grave?*

Davis would have preferred to distance herself from films that capitalized on the actress' recent successes. The title to *Hush ... Hush, Sweet Charlotte* had been changed from "What Ever Happened to Cousin Charlotte?" after Davis requested the title change to differentiate the film so that moviegoers didn't head to the theater thinking they were in for a sequel.

For *Dead Ringer*, Davis plays twin sisters who have been estranged for 20 years after one sister steals the other's one true love. The two are reacquainted at the funeral of the man who split them apart. Margaret DeLorca married the old flame of Edith and got rich, while Edie ended up poor and running a small bar in downtown Los Angeles. Behind in the bills and being kicked out of her home and business, Edie sees Margaret at the funeral, and when Margaret invites her to the mansion, she flaunts her wealth over Edie. Edie soon realizes Margaret never loved her husband and married him only for money, claiming that she was pregnant to trap him. To exact revenge, Edie devises a murderous plot to kill her sister - making it look like her own suicide - and then takes over her sister's life. What she doesn't know is that Margaret and her lover conspired to kill her husband. In taking over the identity of her dead sister she becomes the lead suspect in the murder of the man she loved.

The supporting cast includes Karl Malden as the beat cop who loves Edie, and Peter Lawford as the gigolo Margaret uses to help her commit murder. Estelle Winwood and Jean Hagen also get caught up in the trouble.

If the story sounded familiar for Davis fans, it was. Davis had starred in a similar role of troubled twins in the film *A Stolen Life* in 1946. Bette's co-star from *Now Voyager*, Paul Henreid, was hired as the director for *Dead Ringer*. Henreid recalled, "I understood her temperament and her peculiar gifts ... I knew what she thought was effective for her."

Henreid found the experience a positive one. He had been directing films since 1952 and acting since 1933. He understood both sides of the camera. "Bette had to go through extensive makeup. There was a lot of face-lifting and that sort of thing. But she was a pro. She was always ready. Of all the actors I've ever worked with, Bette was the most professional. I'm talking about acting ability, being on time, cooperating, her attitude, the whole nine yards. Totally professional."

By 1964 Bette Davis was 56 years old and it had been nearly 18 years since she filmed *A Stolen Life*. Playing dual roles, Davis appeared old and matronly as Edie, but spruced herself up as the rich sister Margaret. To pull off the glamorous sister role, Bette needed some Hollywood magic.

Bette recalled that she hadn't actually seen herself onscreen for *Baby Jane* until at the Cannes Film Festival and it brought her to tears seeing herself, "on the screen in all that awful makeup."

She said at the time that she thought to herself, "You sure as hell better get a good-looking part for your next picture or people will really think you look like Jane."

When *Dead Ringer* came along, it was her press agent, Rupert Allen, who suggested that she use straps to tighten and pull back sagging skin to make her appear younger and more attractive. "He introduced me to Gene Hibbs, who used to work for Perc Westmore in the old days at Warners. Gene did makeup tests and used 'lifts' on my face and neck for the first time."

These "lifts" were thin pieces of transparent tape that had adhesive on the ends to stick to the skin. They were placed on the back of the neck, near the ears and at the temples and were attached to rubber bands that could go around the head and draw the skin back off the face and neck, making everything more taut. Makeup and a wig would hide the straps and lifts, taking ten years off her age. Joan Crawford had done the same in her later years on film.

For Bette, it was a necessary, but difficult experience. "Straps are very uncomfortable; you're always aware of them," she said. "And, about three o'clock in the afternoon, you start to perspire under the lights, and your makeup begins to run and the damn things can come undone. If they have a long shooting schedule, your skin gets raw, because the straps have to be glued in the same spots everyday."

For Bette it was worth the agony to show off a more glamorous side of herself. Fans enjoyed seeing her in two roles again when the film was released in February 1964.

However, after the film's release, Bette decided she wanted to avoid using lifts and straps in the future and opted to have a facelift. Ultimately, out of fear of going under the knife, Bette reportedly dropped the idea of a facelift and continued with the lifts and straps to erase the years.

Years later, in 1986, around the time Larry Cohen was crafting his *Wicked Stepmother* script with Bette Davis

in mind, Bette had learned Hollywood was remaking *Dead Ringer*. This time, as a TV movie called *Killer in the Mirror,* the telefilm would star Ann Jillian in the dual role. "Dammit, why can't they leave my old films alone?" complained Bette. "They belong to a certain era."

It was difficult to compare *Dead Ringer* to the host of other screen classics Bette had made that found themselves resurfacing years later, but even so, Bette saw it as an attempt to cash in on her legacy. "I'm not saying *Dead Ringer* was a great picture, but it has a certain flair, technically. A TV budget can't duplicate all those special split-screen effects!" she said.

7

"There was no question that Bette loved my script and wanted to do it."

- Larry Cohen, Writer/Director of *Wicked Stepmother*

Chapter 7

Hush ... Hush, Miss Davis

Studios are reluctant to hire older actors, or actors
with known health problems, because of the steep
price of obtaining insurance against their ability to
complete a film. Nowadays, studios commonly insure even
healthy actors to cover the studio's losses if an actor dies or
becomes ill during production. In the early days, it was not a
common practice and it wasn't really until the 1960s that
insurance became the norm. In Bette Davis' case, Larry Cohen
stated that the insurance company had paid out a $1 million
claim after the star's departure from **Wicked Stepmother,**
and those funds allowed him to complete the picture.
Otherwise, the film would have been shut down.

Years earlier, on the set of **Hush ... Hush, Sweet Charlotte,**
the insurance company demanded that Joan Crawford be
replaced or the picture would be cancelled after Crawford left
the film due to reported illness - though it was suggested that

Crawford was sick at the idea of having to work alongside Bette Davis again. The insurance on Crawford enabled the production to stay afloat until Olivia de Havilland stepped into the part.

...

Joan Crawford was the queen of MGM and for many years, a number one box office star in Hollywood. She was a star who at times shined brighter than any other in Tinseltown. Bette Davis, on the other hand, was the queen of Warner Bros. While her stardom might not have been as lustrous as Crawford's, she was considered the more accomplished actress of the two, whose talent would earn her two Academy Awards. Crawford landed her own Oscar for *Mildred Pierce* in 1945, and would be nominated two additional times. By then the two women were considered fierce competitors. Ironically, Crawford's Academy Award came for a film Bette Davis turned down. While they each shared admiration for the other - their desire to be the better actress and the bigger star made a battle that some suggest would pit the two against one another for their entire careers and the better part of their lives.

By the 1950s both actresses were struggling for survival in Hollywood. As they aged, starlets like Marilyn

Monroe, Elizabeth Taylor, Grace Kelly, and Doris Day were getting the leading lady treatment. Every role that came along required aging actresses like Crawford or Davis to compete against younger actresses and fresher faces to prove themselves as box office draws. For the public was always looking for the next best thing.

Davis had stepped away from the business in the early 1950s to focus on family; to maintain her marriage; and to raise children. She didn't work much during the decade.

Some say that she was content trying to be a good wife and mother. Others suggest she knew that the roles were growing fewer and further between, and figured her willingness to step away from the big screen demonstrated she left by her own choice and not by the choice of the movie makers or the public. However, Bette's life as a successful wife and mother often eluded her.

In contrast, Crawford had left MGM and moved to Warner Bros. only to win an Oscar. During the early 50s, she was still riding high with films like *Johnny Guitar, Sudden Fear, Female on the Beach* and *Queen Bee*. In May 1955, she married for the fourth and final time to Alfred

Steele, chairman of the board for Pepsi-Cola. With four children and a new husband who had a powerful and successful career of his own away from Hollywood, Crawford too began to see a life outside Hollywood. As the wife of an executive she could travel with him and promote Pepsi-Cola using her celebrity status. She too began to look less at making movies and more at making a life for herself. She relocated to New York and designed a Manhattan apartment suitable for a high-powered executive and a movie star.

However, both Davis and Crawford were on a collision course of sorts, and fate would not allow them to live only as happily married wives and mothers. Bette Davis' daughter was diagnosed as mentally disabled in 1954 and while the care was time consuming and difficult, it could also be expensive. She returned to work in *The Virgin Queen* and next in *Storm Center,* but the roles were not as glamorous or as easy to obtain, and she worked only periodically. By the time her marriage fell apart in 1959 she had returned to the stage for work.

Bette Davis and Joan Crawford

WHAT EVER HAPPENED To BABY JANE?

Hollywood was disinterested, and she fought to get cameo parts on TV to make ends meet.

For Crawford, she performed in a few features as well during these times. *Autumn Leaves* and *The Story of Esther Costello* offered suitable roles for a woman her age, but the movies were not as big or lustrous as they had been. However, that was okay until May 1959, when her husband died suddenly of a heart attack. It was difficult enough losing the man with whom she had hoped to spend the rest of her life with, but what was worse was her discovering that he left her with a mountain of debt from loans he had taken out from Pepsi-Cola. "I haven't a nickel. Only my jewels," she told gossip columnist Louella Parsons. "His company did not reimburse me for the half-million dollars I spent on the apartment."

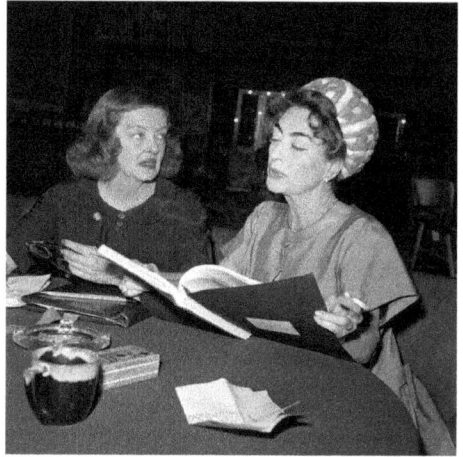

With both actresses without husbands, they became single, working mothers. While that connection might have been something they could have shared, there was little love lost between Bette Davis and Joan Crawford.

However, even without a fondness for one another, Crawford and Davis had a mutual respect for one another and a certain level of envy. Davis always seemed to dislike Crawford, but admired her stardom and beauty, as well as the men she had acquired along the way. On the other hand, Crawford longed for the type of respect and admiration the David had earned from her peers for her acting ability, and always thought Davis was a first-rate talent.

After a small cameo role in Jerry Wald's production of *The Best of Everything,* Crawford returned to Hollywood in 1959, but retained her husband's seat on the Pepsi board and would continue as a spokesperson for the soft drink company.

Davis also needed work, but rejected a role in *The Unforgiven* saying, "I turned it down. I'll be damned if I play Burt Lancaster's mother after 30 years in the business."

However, desperate times called for desperate measures and Davis finally gave in to a supporting role as Apple Annie, a homeless woman who sells apples to Glenn Ford and Hope Lange in *Pocketful of Miracles.* The Frank Capra film would offer a supporting part to Davis, and she hated doing the film, but she needed the paycheck. "I should never have come back to Hollywood," she said in

1976. "I hate all of you! And Apple Annie most of all. I must have been out of my mind to come back here."

Crawford had been looking for a suitable film for her and Davis and *What Ever Happened to Baby Jane?* ultimately proved to be the success for which they were looking - re-launching the careers of both actresses.

The success of the film became a blessing and a curse for both Crawford and Davis, as well as a number of other aging actresses, because it launched what some called a Grand Guignol period for Hollywood horror.

With the hit bringing new life to their careers, it was quickly suggested that the pair continue with another film that could act as a sequel of sorts. Originally called "What Ever Happened to Cousin Charlotte?", the feature was later renamed *Hush ... Hush, Sweet Charlotte,* so that it wouldn't be considered a sequel to the original. While the tale held many similar elements the story would take place in New Orleans and pit cousins against one another in a dark and dreary mansion where murder and lies seem to be all that's left.

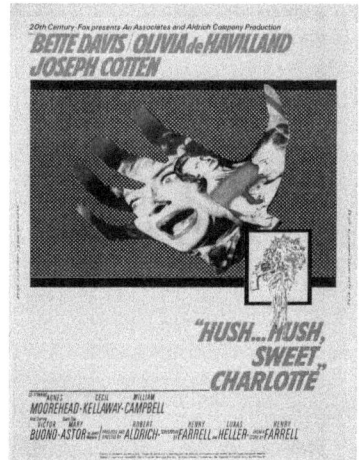

Crawford had suffered a difficult time on the set of *What Ever Happened to Baby Jane?* with Davis looking down on her and creating an atmosphere in which Crawford found difficult to work in. Though the women were professional with each other on the set Davis never hid her personal dislike for her co-star. "Joan and I have never been warm friends," Davis once said. I admire her, yet I feel uncomfortable with her. To me she is the personification of the Movie Star. I have always felt her greatest performance is Crawford being Crawford."

When *Hush ... Hush, Sweet Charlotte* arose, Crawford envisioned the profits that the film would bring her and the opportunity to remain a star on the big screen. However, once on set - and faced with daily combat with Davis - she found that the situation began to get out of hand.

After earning an Oscar nomination for her performance in *Baby Jane*, Davis was still angry at Crawford because she suspected that Crawford had worked against her trying in to get industry insiders to prevent her from winning her third Academy Award. On the set of *Hush ... Hush, Sweet Charlotte*, an incensed Davis worked overtime to turn cast and crew against Crawford and to make her feel like an outsider on a film that she helped bring to life.

Davis didn't want Crawford in the film. Though the two claimed never to have a feud, they never claimed to be friends either. Davis didn't want to share the screen with her again, but only agreed since it was what the studio wanted. And Fox was funding the film - and ultimately Davis's salary. There were rumors that Davis had agreed to co-star with Crawford if they could film their scenes separately - each with a stand-in for the other and the editors could subsequently splice together the footage. Some suggest that the rumor evolved from a joke Davis had made prior to filming.

The original screenplay for *Charlotte* was to be written by Henry Farrell, who had been the author of the novel on which *Baby Jane* was based. However, Farrell was replaced with Lukas Heller, the man who had turned Farrell's *What Ever Happened to Baby Jane?* novel into a screenplay. Davis was reportedly upset with the change and Crawford wasn't pleased with the resulting script.

With the *Charlotte* budget at approximately $1.3 million, shooting began on location in Baton Rouge in on June 4, 1964, and Bette Davis only filmed one scene with Crawford. In the opening sequence, when Davis watches Crawford's character arrive by taxi and enter the aged Louisiana mansion, Crawford and Davis acted together without exchanging a line. No other footage of the two women together was completed. *Life* magazine, however, had a photographer shoot photos of the two stars together, sitting on two gravestones. *Life* never published the photos though, since Crawford failed to complete the picture.

Co-stars in Charlotte included Victor Buono, who was familiar from his work in *Baby Jane*, and Barbara Stanwyck reportedly was offered the role of the slovenly housekeeper Velma. However, Stanwyck exited the role before filming, and Agnes Moorehead assumed the part that would lead her to an Oscar nomination as best supporting actress. For Stanwyck, the exit left her with a contractual obligation for another film and she was reportedly forced to make the 1964 movie *Roustabout* with Elvis Presley. Stanwyck was later approached to replace Crawford on *Charlotte*, but again declined.

Crawford, in turn, took ill during the filming and quickly brought the production to a halt. Initially, they tried

to shoot around her - using her stand-in or filming scenes of which she was not a part - but soon that strategy became difficult. After two weeks of Crawford in the hospital, the film temporarily shut down at the end of June 1964. Crawford returned to the set on July 20, but she could work only sporadically due to her weakened state. "She [Davis] wanted to make a basket case out of Joan, and she almost succeeded," said director George Cukor, who was a friend of Crawford's.

According to *Motion Picture* magazine, during key scenes Bette Davis positioned herself on the set directly in line with the camera and within Crawford's line of sight. During one of Crawford's close-ups Davis was heard saying, "You're not going to let her do it like that, are you?"

When the production moved to Los Angeles for the studio interiors, a delay occurred when Davis was called away for re-shoots on *Where Love Has Gone*. However, by the time she was back Crawford took ill again.

By the end of July, production shut down again to give Joan a chance to fully recover. By August 4, Crawford was back under a doctor's care and unable to work, and the film shut down indefinitely. Some suggest that the fact that Crawford's character is killed by Davis in the climax of the film was one element Crawford found hard to take. Though the plot required such a narrative, some speculated that she refused to finish a film that allowed Bette Davis to "finish her," although it was not all that different from *What Ever Happened to Baby Jane?*

Even though insurance money on Crawford helped keep the production afloat, Davis was beside herself with anger at Crawford's continued absence and quickly began to push to replace her. Soon the producers began approaching other actors to take her place. Katherine Hepburn refused, as did Vivien Leigh. "I can just about stand looking at Joan Crawford's face at six-o'clock in the morning, but not Bette Davis," said Leigh in turning down the role.

Olivia de Havilland was at last approached and she too rejected the film; but after personal pleas from Davis she finally agreed to take part. "I heard the news of my

replacement over the radio, lying in my hospital bed," recalled Crawford. "I wept for 39 hours."

Coming in at a budget near $2 million, the film reportedly grossed $7 million - compared to *What Ever Happened to Baby Jane?* - which cost less than $1 million cost and grossed more than $9 million. Some have suggested that had Davis put the film first and worked with Crawford the film would have fared better at the box office, cost much less, and possibly surpassing *Baby Jane*'s with the two stars reunited.

The *New York Times* called the film "grossly contrived, purposely sadistic, and brutally sickening ... grisly pretentious, disgusting and profoundly annoying. ... Davis accomplishes a straight melodramatic tour de force. Moorehead is allowed to get away with some of the broadest mugging and snarling ever done by a respectable actress ... de Havilland is closer to normal."

Crawford, though upset at being replaced, was also relieved at finally being done with Bette Davis. She had longed to work with the veteran actress and finally got her chance, but it was a heavy price. For both Crawford and Davis the bulk of their work in their later years would resemble versions of *Baby Jane,* though Bette fared better with broader options as the years progressed.

...

Years later, when Larry Cohen approached Bette about doing *Wicked Stepmother* she had believed she had put her horror films behind her. With an Emmy award and a collection of critically acclaimed telefilms, as well as her performance in the art film, *The Whales of August* on her recent resume, Bette had no desire to do a horror film. Cohen, however, crafted a black comedy that alluded to her horrific past and told her he had written the film for her and her alone. She was sold with a chance to have her name back on the marquee and a check for $250,000. What she didn't know was that Cohen had an idea for revisiting Bette's iconic teaming with Joan Crawford and planned to insert her into his film as well. He also had plans to cast her against a young attractive daughter who would bring sex appeal to the black comedy.

8

"We then relaxed together as she generously regaled us with tales of her career, particularly at Warners. How Errol Flynn's trailer would rock visibly back and forth as he entertained young starlets between setups. And how none of the actresses at Warners wanted to do love scenes with Edward G. Robinson."

- Larry Cohen, Writer/Director of *Wicked Stepmother*

Chapter 8

Of Nannies, Domineering Mothers, and Generally Wicked Ladies

*Bette Davis didn't entirely make horror pictures in the 1960s. In addition to television roles she managed a few non-horror roles during these peak years. In addition to 1961's supporting role as Apple Annie in **Pocketful of Miracles,** she had supporting role in **The Empty Canvas,** an Italian drama that received little attention at the box office and less than stellar reviews from the press who covered it. Her other noteworthy feature without a horror angle was released in 1964 by Paramount Pictures. **Where Has Love Gone** was based on a novel of the same name by Harold Robbins. Loosely based on the Lana Turner/Cheryl Crane/Joey Stompanato scandal of 1958, the film had Bette playing the domineering mother of sculptress Susan Hayward, whose daughter is accused of murdering her mother's lover. There was no love lost between Hayward and Davis on or off the set. The two* *suffered each other through the production and had few kind words to say of one another by the time the picture was completed. It was not uncommon for Bette to battle her female costars. Bette accepted the part mainly for the money in order to pay for her daughter B.D.'s wedding to Jeremy Hyman. Bette had agreed to play Susan Hayward's mother for $125,000, even though Bette was only about nine years older than Hayward. Though her hair was grayed to look older, she was dressed in glamorous clothes, fitted with jewels, and given stylish makeup and hair to look regal in the role.*

...

After *Where Has Love Gone*, Bette quickly found her way back toward the darker side of things with 1965's *The Nanny,* a British suspense feature directed by Seth Holt. Starring alongside relative unknowns, Bette plays a supposedly devoted nanny caring for a 10-year-old boy who has recently been discharged from a home for troubled children. Produced by Hammer Film Productions in the United Kingdom, the film was based on a novel of the same name. It capitalized on Bette's recent horror stardom to create the illusion that she was another possible monster like the characters she had played in *What Ever Happened to Baby Jane?* and *Hush ... Hush, Sweet Charlotte.*

Ultimately, the film showed a respectable profit - earning $2.2 million on a budget of $1.3 million. Bette was relatively well received for her portrayal. She reportedly based her performance on several nannies whom she had known over the years and even wore a uniform that she had purchased to give the role authentication after disagreeing on the costume that her producers had selected for the role.

Filming in London and beyond was a pleasant escape for Bette, and she'd always had a strong fan base in the United Kingdom. During production she relaxed in her dressing room after shooting, drinking vodka with her co-star, actress Jill Bennett. Bennett recalled Bette giving her a key piece of advice. "Bette told me, never see your rushes. You'll get depressed about how you look and you won't be able to do a thing about it. I always hated the way I looked onscreen. Bette said she did, too."

Unfortunately for Bette, she failed to heed her own advice years later when viewing her work on *Wicked*

129

Stepmother. Her appearance broke her and nearly broke the film. "I loved Bette. She was real, gutsy, and very dangerous. Dangerous the way a star should be!" said Bennett of working with Bette.

By 1988, Bette was a fraction of her old self. Larry Cohen had managed to sell his concept on her name alone, and MGM offered up $2.5 million for a film with her name on it. According to Cohen, the studio never even met with Davis; and it wasn't until they viewed the work after she had exited the film that they realized what a risk it was.

"They [MGM] didn't get a look at Bette until after shooting began," recalled Cohen. "They started viewing the dailies and as soon as they saw her, they were in complete shock."

The director said MGM executives remarked, "Oh my God, look at her! She's so frail and old," but Cohen was clearly aware of his situation. "It was very sad. I mean this project was a triumph of will power. I wanted to make a movie with Bette, and I insisted I was going to do that ... and I did do it. Even though she eventually left, I made a picture with Bette Davis. Whatever the circumstances were, there are a lot of great directors who can never make that claim."

Cohen prepared for his project by researching his star by viewing of some of her classic pictures, including *The Nanny*. While not Bette's best performance onscreen, it showed a more nuanced, almost cerebral horror. The lack of physical action was also something Davis and Cohen would draw on years later.

The Nanny profited after its theatrical release by selling the TV broadcast rights for $400,000. Fans who failed to see Bette on the big screen would have a chance to see the feature for the first time in a television broadcast. Cohen would find a similar path to Bette's fans years later when a video release enabled him to reach fans after a limited theatrical release failed to ignite the box office.

In some ways scenes from *The Nanny* would resurface in *Wicked Stepmother*. Cohen's original plan was to build a small storyline around Bette and the young son of her stepdaughter and son-in-law. The character Mike would initially find Bette's Miranda a horrific grandmother, but several scenes where Bette uses witchcraft to help him at sports and in school help thaw the ice between the two. Once Davis abandon the picture, only one of the scenes was reworked for Barbara Carrera while several others were eliminated or reduced due to Bette's absence.

WHERE **L**OVE **H**AS **G**ONE

Joseph E. Levine PRESENTS

SUSAN HAYWARD
BETTE DAVIS

CO-STARRING
MICHAEL
CONNORS
JOEY HEATHERTON

Directed By
EDWARD DMYTRYK

TECHNICOLOR

From the novel by
HAROLD ROBBINS...
who wrote the
"THE CARPETBAGGERS"

9

"She complained she never got to play opposite most of the great male stars. Jack Warner knew it wasn't necessary to pay top dollar for a male lead when Bette could carry a movie on her own."

- Larry Cohen, Writer/Director of *Wicked Stepmother*

Chapter 9

The Wicked Mother

B.D. Hyman would never come to terms with the relationship she had with her mother. As the daughter of a star like Bette Davis, she found the role a difficult one - if not entirely impossible. She recalled the first real break in their relationship came in 1963. She said that her mother was so possessive that she wouldn't tolerate her marriage to British film executive Jeremy Hyman, 13 years her senior. B.D. was just 16 at the time.

With Bette being unable to convince her daughter to end the engagement to Hyman, B.D. claimed in a tabloid that Bette placed a "demonic curse" on the couple and that the curse caused the couple's oldest son to develop bipolar disorder. When B.D. was diagnosed with cancer, she considered it another result of her mother's curse. "Mother operated heavily in the occult. Her own mother said she was evil from day one. She loved evil and hated everything nice

and kind and gentle. She did a great many people a great deal
of harm," B.D. reportedly told the tabloid.

B.D. may have mixed Bette's onscreen personas with
her real-life one, but Bette's role as a mother was one of her
greater challenges in life. While she continued to believe she
truly had tried her best to do right by her children, she knew
there was a tradeoff in being an actress - a star - and a mother.
"If your children like you, you can't have been a very good
mother," she told her **Wicked Stepmother** *director, Larry*
Cohen.

A mother with a knack for curses and witchcraft was
just what Cohen had in mind as he crafted his script for
Wicked Stepmother. *Cohen knew Davis had a history of*
playing evil mothers ... and he tailored his story to suit her.

...

Bette's dedication to the role of mother was about as
ill-attempted as Joan Crawford's. While both women had
sought happy marriages and families to lean on outside of
their careers, their focus on themselves, their stardom, and
the work itself made it difficult to commit fully to the
requirements of parenting or the work it takes to make a
successful marriage. Bette gave birth to one child and
adopted two others. It would be years later - just a few

years before her mother would tackle *Wicked Stepmother* - that Bette's natural-born daughter, Barbara Sherry, better known as B.D., would write her own tell-all book about life with Bette Davis. Titled *My Mother's Keeper,* the book was strikingly similar to *Mommie Dearest*, Christina Crawford's tell-all about life as the daughter of Joan Crawford. Bette was incensed and devastated by her daughter's betrayal of her and would never recover from it. If mothering were something at which she had failed, she refused to admit it; and while Joan Crawford was no longer around to defend herself against the accusations in *Mommie Dearest*, Bette came out swinging, with her own book to counter and to respond to B.D.'s accusations. At last, Bette and Joan Crawford indeed had something in common - as Bette saw it ... ungrateful children.

If mothering offscreen was no walk in the park, playing a villainous mother onscreen was something with which Bette she was not only familiar with, but also excelled at it. After playing a mentally unstable governess in *The Nanny*, Bette went full force into the role of troubled mother in the 1968 black comedy, *The Anniversary.*

The Anniversary was originally a play by Bill Macllwraith that had run in London's West End in 1966. Actress Mona Washbourne played the lead role of Mrs. Taggart. Seven Arts, the studio that helped bankroll *What*

Ever Happened to Baby Jane?, partnered with producers at the British film company Hammer Films to bring the play to the big screen. Though approached to star in the theatrical release, Bette actually turned down the role after she had read the initial screen adaptation. However, after working on *The Nanny,* the writer on that film, Jimmy Sangster, offered her a rewrite of the screenplay. Bette responded more favorably to the rewrite and agreed to take the part. Her supporting cast was familiar with the story, having all been involved in the stage production. Sheila Hancock, Jack Hedley, and James Cossins all reprised their stage roles and director Alvin Rakoff was hired to helm the picture.

Trouble started right out of the gate when Bette and Rakoff disagreed on how the film should come together. Bette reportedly said he, "didn't have the first fundamental knowledge of making a motion picture, let alone what an actor was all about."

Rakoff countered Bette's perception by saying that she was, "not the most rational woman one can meet, but a great screen actress. She didn't want a director, she wanted someone enthralled to her."

Roughly a week into production, Rakoff was replaced by Roy Ward Baker. Baker was a seasoned filmmaker with a long list of credits including *The Weaker Sex* (1948), *Don't Bother to Knock* (1952), *A Night to*

Remember (1958), and *Two Left Feet* (1963). Rakoff took his dismissal in stride. "My removal was a mixture of regret and pleasure," he said.

Bette reportedly also wanted co-star Sheila Hancock replaced as well. She reportedly wanted her co-star from *The Nanny*, Jill Bennett, in the role. However, Bennett was unavailable and Hancock remained. Hancock was a veteran of the British theatre and didn't hit it off with the star either. She reportedly resented the attention paid to Bette Davis. "It took me a while to realize this was the way Bette Davis was used to operating. She was a queen, after all," said Hancock.

With her character missing an eye, Bette was required to wear an eye patch for the production. The costume designers created several stylish self-adhesive eye patches for her to wear. She complained that the patch was a "constant irritant" and it reportedly affected her balance, making it difficult for her to walk with it on.

The story takes place during the anniversary party of Mrs. Taggart's marriage to her dead husband where her three sons arrive to celebrate with her. Terry, Henry, and Tom Taggart all work in a construction business owned by their late father. They are dominated their mother, who now runs her late husband's business, making her their boss as well as their mother.

When her son Tom brings his pregnant fiancée to the party and tells his mother that they are planning to marry, she doesn't take the news well. Her son Terry and his wife are secretly planning to leave for Canada to escape his manipulative mother, while the third son Henry turns out to be gay and discovering himself as a transvestite. As the evening progresses, Mrs. Taggart uses every trick she can think of to keep her sons under her control.

Shot at the Elstree Studios in Hertfordshire, the film cost an estimated $1.45 million, but it would earn only about $1.35 million in its U.S. release, failing to deliver the hit for which producers had hoped.

Years later when she read the script to *Wicked Stepmother*, Bette saw similarities to the earlier role. However, her role as a demonic stepmother that she was playing in 1988 was also not entirely unlike the role she was accused of playing concurrently in real life by her daughter B.D. Though Bette might have suspected that portraying an evil stepmother on film wouldn't convince moviegoers she was Mary Poppins in real life, Bette knew that she had a strong fan base and discarded B.D.'s accusations as merely an attempt to cash in on her fame. Bette saw no similarity between herself and the character she had played in the movie.

However, director Larry Cohen inserted a reference to the off-screen Hollywood mothering by inserting a shot of Joan Crawford into his picture as the deceased first wife of Bette's new husband - played by Lionel Stander - in *Wicked Stepmother*. Crawford's image is used by Colleen Camp in a scene where she looks longingly at the picture as she talks about her father's new wife. When Bette saw the scene she took issue with Cohen's tactics.

"Actually, that was not in the original script," recalled Cohen. "When Bette saw that in the dailies, she was very upset. She thought I was trying to put something over on her, I don't know why. I suspect it probably had something to do with *Mommie Dearest*, a book written by Joan Crawford's daughter saying what a terrible person Crawford had been. Bette's own daughter, B.D., then went and wrote a scathing book about her saying what a terrible mother Bette had been. Somehow, a connection had been formed in Bette's mind between the criticism of her own motherhood and the shot of Crawford's photograph. She thought I was making some kind of personal comment on the raising of her child and, of course, I wasn't."

While Cohen meant no harm, he was aware that the gag would be noticed by film fans of Davis and Crawford. The rivalry between the stars appeared to remain, even after Crawford's death, and BD.'s book only made things more painful. "Bette wasn't even on speaking terms with her daughter anymore," said Cohen. "I don't think Bette ever really recovered from the hurt of it. Although I must say, long after that book had been published, and even though the two had been estranged for some years, Bette still had pictures of B.D. on the mantelpiece in her apartment. I guess Bette still harbored hopes of reconciling with her daughter someday."

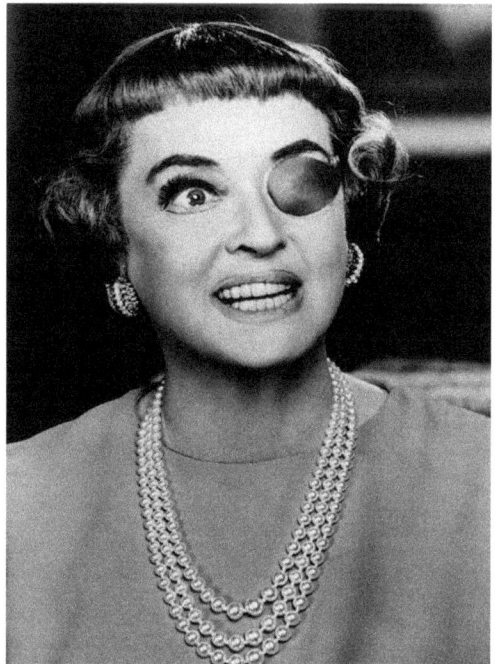

Back in the late 1960s, following on the heels of *The Anniversary,* Bette took on a guest appearance opposite Robert Wagner in his TV series, *It Takes a Thief.* Bette enjoyed working with Wagner so much so that she would work with him again in 1972 in *Madame Sin*. Prior to making *Madame Sin*, though, Bette had landed two feature films roles. While the films were pale comparisons to her work in her heyday, *Connecting Rooms* in 1970 was a European drama with Bette working alongside Michael Redgrave. While the company of actors was strong, the dreary soap opera-like tale offered an uninspired look at the relationships of the residents of a seedy boarding house in London. The film saw little box office and even struggled to find theaters to screen in.

In 1971, Bette starred opposite Ernest Borgnine and Jack Cassidy in *Bunny O'Hare*. The quirky comedy premiered in October with Bette as Bunny, a penniless widow whose house is foreclosed on by a New Mexico bank. She manages to blackmail a robber [Borgnine] after she discovers him looting her home and she talks him into teaching her how to rob banks. After the two team up and embark on a successful crime spree, the cops come calling. The low budget feature was made for less than $1 million.

With a working title "Bunny and Claude," Bunny O'Hare was Bette's second appearance opposite Borgnine. The two had costarred in the lackluster 1956 film *The Catered Affair*. This time, the Oscar winners filmed on location in Albuquerque, New Mexico for exteriors with

some Hollywood soundstage work as well. Borgnine found Bette a true professional to work with, saying, "She was a tiny thing, just 5' 3", and always in motion ... An actress in the 1930s didn't become as big as she was without having some steel in her backbone. But she never, ever used that muscle against her ensemble."

Even though she also found working with Ernest Borgnine a pleasure, Bette was unhappy with the resulting film and sued American International Pictures over edits to the final film. With script approval, Bette claimed the alterations ruined the movie and would result in "damage to her career" resulting in a loss of future income. Bette felt the studio turned the film into a slapstick comedy after she had agreed to star in a film that was intended to be a "social commentary" depicted with humor. The lawsuit would later be dropped, and Bette put the feature behind her. The *New York Times* called the film, "a silly, foolishly entertaining movie ... nonsense of a quite acceptable order, filled with absurd chases and stock characters who have been conceived and played with affection."

Bette, never one to give up after failure, would pick herself up, dust herself off, and move on to the next project. "I had decided, long before most of my contemporaries, that television was going to be a lasting and powerful presence in our lives," she said. "It was the new medium. During those years scripts for 'real films' were hard to come by in Hollywood. You had to accept a different set of rules for television."

The rules indeed were different, but the star - no matter how small the screen - was the same, and she had her own rule book to play by.

10

"She hadn't made a theatrical feature in over 10 years, and her career had been relegated to parts in television movies."

- Larry Cohen, Writer/Director of *Wicked Stepmother*

Chapter 10

Wicked Peggy and a World of Sin

When Bette Davis decided not to return to the set of **Wicked Stepmother** in 1988 there were genuine dental and health issues that prevented her from working. However, Davis - some might say - concocted another story. She claimed the way writer and director Larry Cohen was capturing her on film gave her grave concerns. While it is true that Davis came off looking gaunt and frail, the fact that she was playing a nasty, evil witch might have given her reason to expect her appearance to be horrific. In fact, Davis was no sissy when it came to looking her worst on film. Appearances in **What Ever Happened to Baby Jane?**, **Hush … Hush, Sweet Charlotte**, **The Nanny** and others had her looking matronly, dour, or downright hideous. Davis was even applauded for her bravery.

For **Wicked Stepmother,** however, Davis secretly had issues with how her dialogue broke as she delivered her lines due to an issue with her cracked dentures. This - paired with *her aged appearance - caused her to abandon the film. Instead of using her health as a reason she opted to place blame on her director. Her reason was mainly out of fear that she might never work again. Admitting to health issues would lead future directors, producers, and movie studios to thinking twice about using her. Davis once admitted that if she couldn't act she didn't want to live. So, it stands to reason that she truly believed that there might be a future role for her, if she could explain away her unfortunate venture in accepting the lead in* **Wicked Stepmother***.*

If feature films were beyond her, because the level of commitment was too much for her health to bear, she thought that perhaps a cameo appearance or a TV guest role might come her way, as it had back in the 70s when film roles grew sparse.

...

The 1970s had started off relatively well for Bette in terms of her career. While her film work was not as strong or grand as it had been during her glory years, she was happy to find film and television work to sustain her during her 60s and beyond. "My career not only survived in the 1970s, but grew because of television," she once said.

She hadn't worked since filming *The Anniversary* back in 1967, but in 1970 she saw the spotlight again with a starring role in *Connecting Rooms*. However, the film did little for Bette's career. After a guest appearance on the TV series *It Takes a Thief*, starring Robert Wagner, Bette would re-team with Wagner for the release of the film *Madame Sin*

in 1972. (She would also take part in *Bunny O'Hare* with Ernest Borgnine in 1971.)

Madame Sin was initially planned as a TV movie pilot for a weekly series on ABC TV. However, when the pilot failed to make the network schedule for 1971-72 TV season, the network opted to air it as a stand-alone telefilm. Broadcast in January 1972 in the U.S., the film was repackaged and released later as a feature film internationally. Bette starred an Asian villainess who runs an evil "Thought Factory" in Scotland. In a quest for world domination, she kidnaps an ex-CIA agent named Anthony Lawrence, played by Robert Wagner, forcing him to help her steal a submarine that happens to have a nuclear weapon on board.

Bette said it was pleasure working with Wagner because even though he was young, he had experienced the "customs of old Hollywood." So, when she arrived on the set of his series, she was greeted with a lovely dressing room with her name, "Miss Bette Davis" on the door and flowers on her makeup table. "I recall Robert beautiful ... and that he is - inside and out," she said of working alongside him.

In 1973, Bette Davis' horror film career went where it never had gone before - to television. *Scream, Pretty Peggy* was a television horror film directed by Gordon Hessler and starred Bette alongside *That Girl*'s Ted Bessell. Shot on an estate just above the Sunset Strip in Hollywood, the telefilm follows a young college student who is given a job as a housekeeper at a mysterious mansion where her employer's sister and elderly mother reside. Broadcast by ABC on November 24, 1973, the horror-suspense story was called a "routine shocker" and did little to boost Bette's sagging career.

Bette wouldn't recall the picture fondly when she considered it amongst her many other projects. "I have never hesitated to admit when a film I made was junk," she said of the film. "In the final analysis, a good picture cannot be harmed, nor a poor one helped, by the size of the screen. In 1973, I costarred with Ray Milland in an ABC Movie of the Week called *Scream, Pretty Peggy.* The film had a Peggy in it, but no screams - except for my silent ones."

Bette filmed the telefilm in the spring of 1973, but elements of the project irritated her and she let her frustration be known. Director Gordon Hessler had decided that the best way to make his TV movie was to film it chronologically. This strategy meant filming the script in order as the story progressed. It's rarely done in filmmaking because it can be costly and put more pressure on the cast and crew. Most often, the more sensible way is to use common sets and locations at the same time, so camera set-ups, lighting, and actors can be utilized and then moved for the next set of scenes. Though the film was entirely shot at a mansion above the Sunset Strip, the large estate meant shooting on various floors as well as inside and outside the house. This scenario required the crew to move vast amounts of equipment around the location, slowing production and angering the star.

The mansion used in the film had been owned by Noah Dietrich, an American businessman, who had been the chief executive officer of the Howard Hughes business empire from 1925 to 1957. His Hollywood mansion was eerie and foreboding enough to create the sinister atmosphere for the film, but the vastness of it made set-up of the filming challenging. "The production is running needlessly behind schedule," Bette complained to production executives. "Why can't Hessler shoot all our scenes that take place in the same room, and then go on to the next location like we usually do?"

However, Bette was merely a special guest star in the production, being paid roughly $15,000 for a supporting role of an aging mother troubled by her son, who happens to be a transvestite. The network hoped that the *Psycho* backstory and a horror legend like Bette would pull in fall sweeps ratings. Her requests were acknowledged but did little to change the production. The 74-minute film eventually aired on Saturday night, November 24, 1973 at 8:30 p.m., but had a hard time competing against competition from top 10 CBS network shows *M*A*S*H* and *Mary Tyler Moore*.

While *Scream, Pretty Peggy* utilized Bette's well-established horror heritage, the star made two other telefilms during the same period that gave her a chance to escape the genre that largely defined her later years. The *Judge and Jake Wyler* in 1972 and while *Hello Mother, Goodbye*, bookended her *Peggy* offering.

Bette wasn't sure if she had another feature film in her future, but she continued to search for the right project. Fortunately for Bette, her forays into horror would offer her another shot at the big screen.

11

"When visitors dropped by our location, Bette gladly spent time with them, signed autographs, and seemed pleased to be in their company. Although she had an elaborate dressing room, she insisted on coming to the set early and having a chair placed in the midst of the crew who were balanced above her on ladders hanging lights. She usually situated herself in the most precarious spot."

- Larry Cohen, Writer/Director of *Wicked Stepmother*

Chapter 11

The Offerings Were Burnt

B ack in the 1940s, Tallulah Bankhead was a legend on the stage. Her screen credits were not as long, but her personality was equal or even larger than many of her contemporaries. Bette Davis was possibly the exception. In many ways Davis and Bankhead were branded similar talents. Without chorus girl good looks or figures, both women relied purely on their talent and acting chops to stay at the top of their game. When roles requiring just such an actress were being cast, they were often up against one another for parts.

During much of their prime years, stories of a feud between the two persisted. As Bankhead landed **Dark Victory** and **The Little Foxes** on the stage, it was Davis who was handed the big screen roles. When **What Ever Happened to Baby Jane?** was being cast it was rumored that Bankhead was one of the screen legends considered for the part that Joan Crawford would ultimately play.

Bette often found rivals in other leading ladies, and feuds were nothing new. Bankhead was convinced that Davis spread lies about her to the press, once remarking, "Don't think I don't know who's been spreading gossip about me and my temperament out there in Hollywood - where that film was made - 'All About Me'. And after all the nice things I've said about that hag. When I get a hold of her, I'll tear out every hair of her mustache!"

*Bette would continue to have trouble with her fellow actresses, including Faye Dunaway on **The Disappearance of Aimee** and Karen Black in **Burnt Offerings**. By the late 1980s most of her contemporaries were either retired or dead. There were few feuds to be had.*

...

In June 1975, Bette was in need of work. While she still wanted to live like the star of yesteryear her income wasn't what it once was.   She hadn't done a film since 1972 with parts in *Madame Sin* and a small Italian film called *The Scopone Game*. However, neither film was huge box office, or paid much of a star salary. Though she felt lucky with the work and income from *The Judge and Jake Wyler* (1972), *Scream, Pretty Peggy* (1973) and *Hello Mother, Goodbye* (1974), she was frustrated that she wasn't in higher demand.

When Dan Curtis approached her with a role in a new horror film, she thought maybe things were turning around. However, when she learned she'd be playing a small supporting role as Aunt Elizabeth; and the leads would be Karen Black and Oliver Reed, she had to swallow her pride and once again do it for the paycheck.

Dan Curtis was primarily a TV producer whose main claim to fame was as executive producer of the TV soap opera *Dark Shadows* in the late 60s and early 70s. In addition to the series, most of his other work was also horror related and focused on the small screen. Telefilms like *The Night Strangler, The Night Stalker, The Picture of Dorian Gray, Dracula,* and *Scream of the Wolf* were some of his recent efforts. Curtis would be credited as both co-writer, director, and a producer of *Burnt Offerings*.

"I told Curtis that I wouldn't even consider the script if I disappeared in a sneeze, and he assured me I wouldn't," recalled Bette of her part in *Burnt Offerings*.

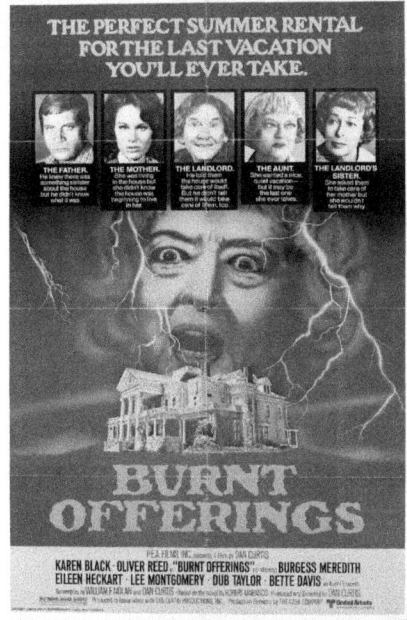

159

Spending most of her time at her home in Westport, Connecticut, Bette traveled to the West Coast for the Los Angeles shoot. She stayed at The Bel Air Hotel, her usual haunt when in Hollywood for work. The property was originally built on a 600-acre plot of land in 1922 to serve as the estate and planning offices for the new community of Bel Air. In 1946, it was converted into a hotel after 18 acres were acquired by hotel entrepreneur Joseph Drown. With 100 rooms, the hotel featured 45 suites which were long-coveted by Hollywood stars in search of privacy. Bette liked the fact that you could enter and exit the suite without having to traipse through the lobby. The property was just a short distance from her former home, so she knew the area well. The Mission-style façade in West Los Angeles featured a small lake, which guests crossed by foot bridge to get to the hotel. The grounds were covered with lush gardens of continuously-blooming flowers and were lined with ficus, fig, and palm trees. From here, she managed soundstage work before heading to the Pacific Northwest for location shooting.

Bette described the film to writer Whitney Stine over lunch at the hotel one afternoon in the summer of 1975. "I play an old auntie, fairly normal. It's a spooky, supernatural story of the effects that an old house has on a family of renters. They all have personality changes, and the house becomes newer and newer, I become older and older. It's not strictly a horror picture, although I have a smashing death scene - if the damned thing comes off. It's not a film I would choose to do, but at this point I want to keep working."

Location shooting took the actors north in August 1975, to the Dunsmuir House in Oakland, California. During the filming the actors stayed at the same hotel. Bette complained of co-star Oliver Reed's noisy, drunken evenings because he kept waking her up in the middle of the night when he returned to his room, which was next to hers.

Bette also had little positive to say about leading lady Karen Black, calling her "unprofessional." Some suggest

the dislike of her co-stars came from the fact that Davis felt her fellow actors did not pay her the appropriate level of respect to which she felt she was entitled. Bette said that Black "changes her makeup in the middle of a scene so nothing matches on the screen. She sleeps all day; never goes to rushes and you can't hear a bloody thing she says on the set. When I made movies, you could hear me in a tunnel!"

Bette did manage to get decent billing in the film even though she's not featured in much of it. She recalled the filming was difficult, and people felt superstitious about the production. Dan Curtis' daughter would kill herself by throwing herself out of a window during the filming, and the feature had to shut down for a period. Ironically, when they returned, the filmmakers had to film Oliver Reed being thrown from a window to his death in the climax of the movie. "It definitely tainted things," said Bette.

The Dunsmuir House played as much a character in the film as the actors. The foreboding house was built in 1899 and sits on 50-acres of ground. Built by a wealthy coal magnate named Alexander Dunsmuir, the house featured Neoclassical-Revival architecture and suited the gothic story well. Dunsmuir's story did as well. It's owner came to the San Francisco Bay area in 1878 and built the house as a wedding gift for his new bride. Unfortunately, he became ill and died during his honeymoon in New York and never got to live in the house. His new bride would return to live in the home, but would die in 1901.

Film critic Roger Ebert said, "*Burnt Offerings* just persists, until it occurs to us that the characters are the only ones in the theater who don't know what's going to happen next."

Variety wrote, "The horror is expressed through sudden murderous impulses felt by Black and Reed, a premise which might have been interesting if director Dan Curtis hadn't relied strictly on formula treatment."

Though the film did little to boost Bette's career she was delighted to learn she was named the winner of the Best Supporting Actress award for her *Burnt Offerings* performance by the Academy of Science Fiction, Fantasy & Horror Films in 1977. Other horror features like *The Omen* and *Carrie* fared better at the box office; and features like *Network, All the President's Men, Marathon Man,* and Alfred Hitchcock's final film, *Family Plot,* offered more drama and suspense to moviegoers that year. Bette longed to work in first-rate pictures like those.

After the film's release, Bette offered her assessment of the final result. "It's such a hideous mess!" she exclaimed. "God, if I didn't need the money! *Jane* was fine,

Charlotte was great, and *Nanny* was okay, but dear god, I can't keep on playing these crazies!"

However, roughly a decade later, Bette would be back on the horrific bandwagon - though in a black comedy spoof of her years in horror. When she took on the lead in *Wicked Stepmother,* she'd long forgotten about her work in *Burnt Offerings.*

12

"If I had to do it all again I would, because I enjoyed having Bette as an acquaintance and having her at least appear to like me."

- Larry Cohen, Writer/Director of *Wicked Stepmother*

Chapter 12

Wicked on a Mountain

B*ette Davis had legendary, knock down drag out fights with most of her directors or producers. Several even led to legal issues and court proceedings against her. Bette often looked to go public and get her fans on her side. Whether it was Jack Warner or the power brokers at Warner Bros., arguments with Irving Rapper on **Now Voyager**, Robert Aldrich on **Hush ... Hush, Sweet Charlotte,** Edward Dmytryk on **Where Has Love Gone**, she was never one to shy away from confrontation.*

*So, it's no surprise that as **Wicked Stepmother** took shape, Bette - who saw herself as a legend and an icon who knew more about the movies than most of her directors - would look to wreak havoc on Larry Cohen and the production of **Wicked Stepmother**, if for no other reason than it was good publicity for her, and a chance to lay blame anywhere other than on herself for the quality of the work.*

...

"Growing old is hell," Bette once said. "If I was just a housewife, I wouldn't mind; but it's going out in public that gets on my nerves. People who've just seen you on television the night before in *Victory* or *Voyager* or *Eve* expect you to look the same, and sometimes you can see the disbelief in their faces."

As Bette neared 70 years old, what few glamour years she had possessed were far behind her. While glamorous roles were few and far between, she enjoyed being dolled up to look her best on screen, but wasn't beneath creating an ugly persona, if it were right for the film. However, as she aged, she became more concerned about appearing old and avoided dressing down when possible. Even when going out in public, she always made a point of making sure she looked like the movie star she was. It was something she had in common with her old nemesis, Joan Crawford, who receded from public life after seeing her aged self in a newspaper after an event in the early 1970s.

In 1975, Disney's *Escape to Witch Mountain* was a box office hit pulling in some $20 million from families who bought tickets to see a pair of orphaned siblings discover extraordinary psychic powers and find themselves up against grownups while uncovering the truth behind their powers. The success would result in a sequel; and in the role of one of the villains, Bette was offered a starring part.

In many ways, the role wasn't really a lead role at all, with Bette co-starring alongside horror icon Christopher Lee and a few teenage actors. Her role in fact was fairly minimal, but her name was a big enough draw that the producers listed her as the star of the film.

The story centers on a teenage sister and brother with extraordinary powers who leave their safe haven on Witch Mountain to travel to Los Angeles. When the boy is kidnapped by an evil Dr. Gannon and his spinster partner Letha (Davis), he is implanted with a mind control chip in order to help the evil pair commit a series of crimes. It's up to his sister and friends to rescue him.

For Bette, the role was an unimagined one, but it was an opportunity to reach a new audience. At various times in her career, including her foray into horror for *What Ever Happened to Baby Jane?* (1962), Bette realized that the genre would introduce her to a legion of potential new fans who were unfamiliar with her work in features like *Jezebel, The Little Foxes*, and *All About Eve*. She had never worked in a Disney picture and knew that the children who would see her onscreen weren't even born when she filmed *Baby Jane*.

Actors like Ray Milland and Eddie Albert had worked in the first film; and with Lee working alongside her, she likely felt that there was something to be said in taking the role. Aside from the paycheck, she also believed that Disney had the funding and the skills to create a top-notch film.

The film offer came at a great time for Bette. Aside from the fact that her offers were coming less frequently, work in 1977 was important, because it showed that she was still actively working in her craft. All the more important, it was announced that in March 1977 that Bette would be the first woman honored with the American Film Institute's Lifetime Achievement Award. The star would appear onstage to accept the award for her career and be lauded by her peers for a job well done. To be able to accept the award while still working and due on the set of her next film not long after receiving the award, meant a great deal to the leading lady.

Shortly after the lifetime achievement award ceremony, Bette returned to New York to rest and to prepare for her next feature. A few months later, she was back in Hollywood for soundstage work on the Disney picture. "They treat you wonderfully at Disney," she told friend and writer Whitney Stine. "A very pleasant atmosphere to work in, and the money is good and I just may reach an untapped audience out there. Children, for obvious reasons, are not drawn to my pictures. I usually don't attract them until puberty, and sometimes beyond!"

It was in the spring when she arrived at the Sheraton Hotel to a comfortable ninth-floor mini-suite. From her window she overlooked the entrance to Universal Studios. Gone was the façade she remembered, but it was nostalgic nonetheless, recalling to friends how she was fired from the studio not long after having gotten there. Beyond Universal, she could also make out part of the Warner Bros.

lot, a place she called home for decades by landing on her feet after her exit from Universal.

It was like coming home for the star. She had the chance to catch up with some old friends, like photographer George Hurrell, and to pass by the former home which she shared with husband Arthur Farnsworth in 1939. She also took time to visit her mother's grave at Forest Lawn Cemetery in the Hollywood Hills.

Bette had mixed feelings toward her Disney director John Hough. She called him an "instinctive director," because he didn't have everything mapped out by the time she arrived. It left uncertainty and spontaneity that she failed to appreciate after 50 years in the business.

As for playing the part, she went through the motions, but didn't see much challenge to it. "I play a kind of funny villainess, Letha Wedge, and I am going to look as good as I can, no horrible death scenes. My leading man is Christopher Lee. He's very menacing in the script. If this picture is ever remembered, it will not be because of me, but the special effects - things flying through the air ..."

Since Bette refused to look anything less than her best, cinematographer Frank Phillips had to shoot her like other directors had done on her recent projects. He placed "fill light" in from the camera to soften her close-ups. The high-key color film photographed her best when the light flooded her face and filled in her wrinkles. Bette was satisfied with the results.

One of the biggest disagreements Bette had on the picture was in shooting the climax of the movie. For the scene, Bette and Christopher Lee were suspended high in the air on scaffolding and the director requested that she climb into position for the scene. "I'm not a stunt woman! I won't get up there," she bellowed back.

"I'd rather not use a double, it will be too obvious," said Hough.

"To hell with you," she replied. "Get together with the cameraman to work out the angle."

Hough would ultimately use a stuntwoman for the scene, having her grasp rope and use her arms and the scaffolding to hide her face to give the illusion that the star was up in the air.

Bette was happy when the film was over; however, she found that newer ways of making films was getting beyond her. "It would be more Gothic if it was shot in black and white," she complained. "The beautiful part about makeup for black and white films is that you can use all the shades of gray. For instance, there was never a color picture made that could really show devastating illness. Everything is prettified."

Even so, Bette cashed the check and was happy to find that she'd once again be back on the big screen. *Return from Witch Mountain* was released in December 1977 to mediocre reviews. *Variety* took notice of the special effects, but it had little to say about the performances. Another review found that, "Both Davis and Lee are slumming it big time," but added that they "ham it up every step of the way and in the process manage to add some fun to the otherwise weak script."

The film would pull in more than $16 million at the box office, making it a legitimate success for the aging star.

In fact, it would be one of her best-performing films in theatrical release in the 1970s and for the remainder of her career.

Burt Reynolds, who became friends with Davis in her later years, found that she had crossed into a pop-culture icon status by the 1980s. No matter how good she was - or how bad the film was - she was still Bette Davis. "Bette had the ability to make you believe in the character she was playing while never forgetting you were watching Bette Davis," said Reynolds. "She was always interesting on the screen, even if she was pushing a peanut up a hill with her nose. She wasn't afraid to play unattractive characters; parts other actresses wouldn't touch - parts that were dangerous and hard to bring off: killers, connivers, ugly ducklings."

In many ways, Bette's later work in films like *Return from Witch Mountain* would form the character she would build on for *Wicked Stepmother.* Along with references to *What Ever Happened to Baby Jane, The Nanny,* and *The Anniversary,* her character's interactions with other family members were aligned with roles she was very familiar with.

13

"[W]hen visitors dropped by our location, Bette gladly spent time with them, signed autographs, and seemed pleased to be in their company."

- Larry Cohen, Writer/Director of *Wicked Stepmother*

Chapter 13

Back in Her Wheelhouse

Bette Davis had starred in the film ***John Paul Jones*** *in 1958 and her director was John Farrow, father of Mia Farrow. During location filming in Madrid, both Mia and Bette's daughter B.D. were with their parents, and because the girls were both about the same age they became friends. Bette got to know Mia as she took the girls sightseeing and spent time with her when not filming. Years later, Bette said Mia visited her on the set of **Hush ... Hush, Sweet Charlotte** and she was taken back to see Mia all grown up and pursuing a career in acting. She was proud of the woman Mia had become.*

Several years later, Bette said Mia came to her for advice on marrying Frank Sinatra. Bette warned not to do it if it meant having to give up her career. Mia married Sinatra anyway, but the marriage would end in divorce as Bette suspected.

*Years would go by, but the two would occasionally be in touch. When they had the chance to work together on **Death on the Nile**, Bette was delighted to share the screen with her. "It was fun to work with her, and Mia was sort of a daughter to me."*

...

If Bette had hopes that *Wicked Stepmother* would be a grand affair, she soon realized that it was not to be. With the production budget limited; the cast void of major star names; and a lack of picturesque production settings; Larry Cohen's feature would be made largely in one place, with capable actors, and on a shoestring. Bette had to hang onto yesteryear for the grand days of moviemaking. Still, she enjoyed being on a movie set, even if in awkward or uncomfortable situations.

Larry Cohen recalled her desire to be right in the middle of all the action. While she would suffer with those whom she didn't like or respect - and would be more than willing to put them in their place when she disagreed with them - she wanted to be a part of everything. "Although she had an elaborate dressing room, she insisted on coming to the set early and having a chair placed in the midst of the crew who were balanced above her on ladders hanging lights. She usually situated herself in the most precarious spot."

In reality, most of Bette's recent work was on a smaller scale. With much of it in television, Bette was accustomed to a handful of days' work on a small set at a lower salary than she had commanded at the height of her career. The last really major screen feature on which she worked on was back in 1978, when she appeared as part of an all-star cast in *Death on the Nile*.

After receiving her lifetime achievement honors from the American Film Institute, Bette had hoped the film offers would come flooding in. However, she was disappointed when little came her way. With *Death on the Nile,* she had finally landed something good.

Agatha Christie's 1937 novel would get its big screen adaptation in 1978. Directed by John Guillermin, the film featured a murder mystery being investigated by the

Belgian detective Hercule Poirot, played by Peter Ustinov. To deliver on a popular all-star cast that was prevalent in the 1970s, a collection of name actors including Maggie Smith, Angela Lansbury, Mia Farrow, David Niven, George Kennedy and Jack Warden were cast. Bette was invited to appear along with the other stars as one of the prime suspects.

After the success of a 1974 all-star cast version of Christie's *Murder on the Orient Express,* the producers quickly set their sights on another picture. *Death on the Nile* was shot over seven weeks on location in Egypt in the latter months of 1977. With filming in Aswan, Abu Simbel, Luxor, and Cairo, the work was long and hot for the cast and crew. Filming in the desert reportedly started at 4 a.m. with shooting underway by 6 a.m. because temperatures

climbed to nearly 130 degrees by noon. Filming would be suspended until the sun was setting and things cooled down. Bette was taken back by the strenuous shoot, including the fact that no hotel reservations had been made for the cast and crew, and they had to change hotels on several occasions. Bette told one interviewer, "In the older days, they'd have built the Nile for you. Nowadays, films have become travelogues and actors, stuntmen."

Though the film had challenges, it was reported that since the cast and crew had years of experience, it made things run more smoothly than it might have otherwise.

Death on the Nile premiered in New York in September 1978, around the opening of a traveling exhibition "The Treasures of

Tutankhamun" at the New York Metropolitan Museum of Art. It was hoped that interest in King Tut and the collection of Egyptian artifacts would draw moviegoers to the picture. It then premiered in London in October. At a cost of nearly $8 million to produce, the film turned a nice profit after earning more than $14.5 million at the box office. However, it was a far cry from *Murder on the Orient Express*, which was made on a budget of less than $2 million and earned more than $35 million.

Even so, Bette was proud of the work and the quality film. She hadn't had many quality experiences in recent years, but this was one of the better features. While it wasn't a starring role, it was a decent part in good film and for that she could be grateful.

In addition to the 1978 feature film, Bette would bookend the movie with two TV projects. *The Dark Secret of Harvest Home* was a two-part miniseries about a family that moves to a New England town only to be caught up in secrets, lies and spooky goings on. It would air on NBC in January 1978, and it would capitalize on Bette's past affiliation with her collection of horror films. *Strangers: The Story of a Mother and Daughter* would air in May 1979 and would star Gena Rowlands as a woman who returns home after 20 years - after learning she is terminally ill - in order to heal old wounds with her mother. Bette would co-star as

Rowlands' mother and would find her work would be nominated for the Emmy for Outstanding Lead Actress in a Limited Series or a Special. "I wanted to badly win that Emmy," she said of her nomination. "I felt I deserved it, if not for the performance I gave, then for the difficulty of the part and the hardships of the filming. The setting was a Rhode Island summer, but we worked in the bitter winter cold of Montecito, in Northern California."

Though Bette was unable to attend the awards ceremony, she was delighted to learn she had won the

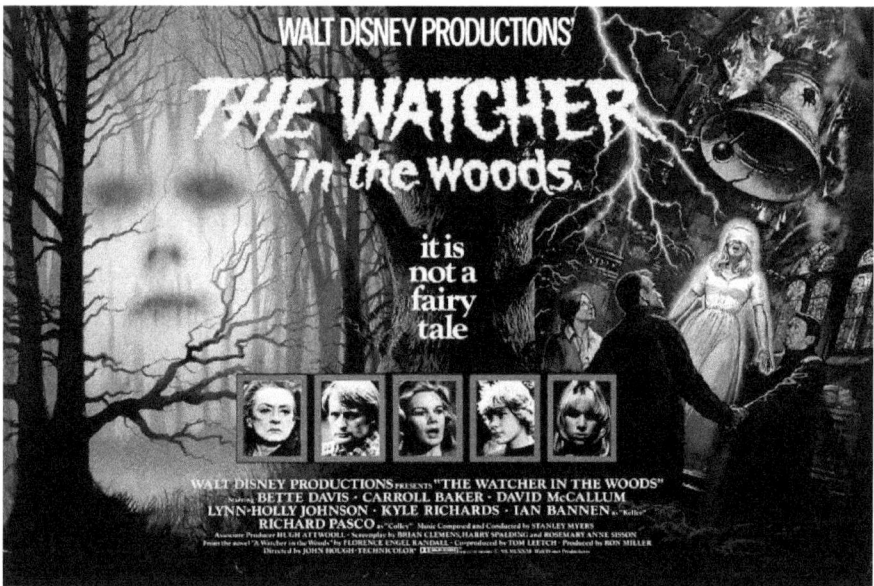

Emmy for Outstanding Lead Actress. It was her first and only Emmy award. She'd been nominated once before in

1974 and would go on to earn two more nominations, but she would never again walk away with the coveted honor.

When the awards night came, she was off filming her next feature, *Watcher in the Woods*.

14

"She got into the habit of phoning me day or night with any thoughts that she might have at the moment, quickly stating an opinion then hanging up without even saying goodbye."

- Larry Cohen, Writer/Director of *Wicked Stepmother*

Chapter 14

Wicked in the Woods

In the spring of 1989 Bette Davis was one of several veteran actors featured on the cover of **Life** magazine. The edition featured a film retrospective celebrating the films and stars of 1939. **Life** named Davis as the "most significant actress of her era," highlighting **Dark Victory** (1939) as one of the most important films of the year. Appearing on the cover in a photograph with James Woods, Bette was celebrated along with James Stewart, Olivia de Havilland, and Don Ameche as one of the legends still making waves in Hollywood. Bette was reportedly friends with Woods, after having worked with him on the 1976 telefilm **The Disappearance of Aimee**.

...

As the 1980s came into view, the movie roles were hard to come by for an aging star like Bette. *Death on the*

Nile had been her last feature film; and though it was a relatively strong film with a quality role, unfortunately, it didn't lead to a deluge of other offers. She did land enough work on TV to keep her busy until 1979, when *The Watcher in the Woods* came her way.

Based on a 1976 novel by Florence Engel Randall, *The Watcher in the Woods* tells the story of a teenage girl and her little sister living in the English countryside who are caught up in a mystery surrounding another missing girl in the wooded area near their home. The girls become immersed in supernatural activities and the occult as events from the past impact their present. In a supporting role, Bette plays Mrs. Aylwood, the mother of the missing girl.

Not unlike her work several years earlier in the film *Return to Witch Mountain*, this would be another opportunity to reach a younger audience. Filmed at Pinewood Studios and nearby Buckinghamshire, England,

The Watcher in the Woods was another live-action film produced by Walt Disney Productions.

Bette traveled with her assistant Kathryn Sermak, and stayed at the Berystede Hotel in Ascot. Though Bette had star-billing, the role actually wasn't a very large one. "The part was a short one," recalled Bette. "I worked only some ten days in the six weeks we were there, and actually had time to prune the geraniums daily in the garden at the inn where we stayed."

"You couldn't play a scene with Bette Davis and not really think and not be on your toes, as you just wouldn't have any impact on the scene at all," said director John Hough of working with Davis on the film. Hough noted that the casting for the role of a younger Mrs. Aylwood was complicated, with the character featured in two separate time periods. Bette took on the role of the older Mrs. Aylwood, and reportedly wanted to play the younger part as well, but Hough didn't feel she could pull it off.

To placate her, Hough had a make-up artist and hair stylist flown in from Los Angeles to prepare Bette for a screen test for the younger part. The hope was to cut decades off her appearance. However, by the end of the day Hough felt that the make-up and hair work had, "maybe knocked about twenty years off of her age, but not forty."

Bette, who was 72 years old at the time, sat down with Hough in the screening room after the lights went up. "Bette, I don't think you've made it."

Taking a long drag from her cigarette, she replied, "You're goddamn right."

Georgina Hale was then hired on for role of the young Mrs. Aylwood.

The film premiered at the Ziegfeld Theatre in New York City in April 1980, but was yanked from release after just ten days due to negative reaction from audiences. Future screenings were canceled by the studio after critics blasted the film. Disney producers took to reworking the film before trying again with audiences.

Several key changes were made, including cuts to a pre-credit sequence and the filming of an entirely new ending. Due to a 1980 actors' strike, Bette was unable to

return to England for reshoots; so, her additional footage had to be shot in California. With John Hough unavailable, the new ending was directed by Vincent McEveety, though his efforts would go uncredited.

Disney tried to promote the film as a new and unique film with the tagline, "Walt Disney Productions ushers in a new decade of motion picture entertainment with the following invitation to spend ninety minutes on the edge of your seat."

Reworking did little to help the film. The studio re-released the revised 84-minute version of the film 18 months later on October 9, 1981, but it grossed only $5 million, losing some $4 million after the budget topped out at a reported $9 million by the time the feature was completed.

Though critical response to the performances was mixed, the majority of the reviews were unfavorable. However, in the years since, *Watcher in the Woods* has garnered a cult following, including many loyal Davis fans - not unlike her final film *Wicked Stepmother.*

15

"Taking note of her furnishings, I focused on an embroidered cushion that lay on her sofa. The lettering read: 'Old age is not for sissies.' Bette might as well have been a poster girl for this slogan."

- Larry Cohen, Writer/Director of *Wicked Stepmother*

Chapter 15

Best Laid Plans

If the norm for Bette Davis was to have difficulty costarring alongside other strong actresses, her 1983 work in the TV movie, **Murder With Mirrors**, proved to be an exception. While Davis was long for criticizing nearly every fellow actress with whom she crossed had paths - from Joan Crawford to Karen Black, Faye Dunaway, Tallulah Bankhead and more - there were the rare occasions that she found a woman with whom she could work. Olivia de Havilland was one. Another would turn out to be Helen Hayes.

Murder With Mirrors would be filmed in 1984, and aired on TV in February 1985. Based on the Agatha Christie novel of the same name, Hayes would take on the main role as Miss Jane Marple, with Bette playing her old friend who is apparently being poisoned with arsenic.

Bette was still recovering from a stroke and other ailments when she traveled to England for the production shoot. She was grateful for the work, considering her health scare, and found Hayes to be a breath of fresh air compared to other past co-stars. "*Many years before, Helen Hayes, as the 'First Lady' of American Theatre, visited the set where I was filming* **The Sisters.** *I was thrilled when she complimented me on my work.*"

Perhaps, it was due to the fact that Hayes was far more established in the theater and less in film that Bette didn't see her as a threat. "*I was a bit in awe working with Miss Hayes, I must say. And she confided later that she was also uneasy about working with me,*" she said.

"*In effect,* **Murder with Mirrors** *was my return to the world of the living,*" Bette would ultimately remark of the film.

...

If the 1980s were lean years for feature films, Bette's shortage of work on the silver screen led her to the small screen and TV was only too happy to have her. *White Mama* would be her first telefilm project of the decade, airing in March 1980. Bette would portray an elderly woman living in a tough city neighborhood. She becomes friends with a local poor boy, and the two form a strong bond that provides her both companionship and protection. She in turn becomes a mother figure he is missing. Bette found herself nominated for an Emmy for Outstanding Lead Actress in a Limited Series or a Special for her work in the telefilm.

In *Murder with Mirrors,* Bette costarred opposite Helen Hayes and Sir John Mills. Mills said of working with her, "I was never so scared in my life. And I was in the war!"

Helen Hayes also found the project a challenge, contrary to Bette's recollections. She would later claim the difficult experience was one of the reasons she stopped working.

Watcher in the Woods would premiere on the big screen in New York City, but reviews would cause the film to be pulled for re-working and wouldn't reappear until fall. By then her next telefilm, *Skyward,* would be ready to hit TV screens in November. In the TV movie, Bette would play and aging flight instructor who signs up to teach a young girl confined to a wheelchair how to fly. She would be amused that her director, Ron Howard, was best known for roles as the youngster she remembered from *The Andy Griffith Show* and *Happy Days*.

Three more TV movies would keep her busy when she appeared in *Family Reunion* which aired in October 1981; *A Piano for Mrs. Cimino* airing in February 1982; and *Little Gloria … Happy at Last* airing in October 1982. The

latter would co-star Angela Lansbury, Maureen Stapleton
and Martin Balsam and detail Gloria Vanderbilt's troubled
childhood and the bitter custody battle between her
mother and her aunt. Both Bette and Angela Lansbury
would be nominated for Emmys for Supporting Actress, but
neither would win the award.

In October 1982 Bette began filming *Right of Way*
with Jimmy Stewart as her co-star. HBO produced the film
with hopes that teaming the screen legends would remind
viewers of the teaming of Katharine Hepburn and Henry
Fonda in the Oscar-winning *On Golden Pond*. Unfortunately,
the film about an elderly couple who are determined to
commit suicide against the wishes of their daughter, did not

live up to expectations. Reports suggest that although Stewart never admitted it publicly, privately he did not enjoy working with Davis. According to Stewart's wife Gloria, "She thought the film was only about her," she said. "She didn't give Jim a chance."

In one scene where Stewart was supposed to give Davis a kiss, Davis refused. "When Jim went to kiss her, she turned her head away. Everyone was shocked, especially Jim. So in the next take he just hugged her."

Gloria Stewart believed Bette's ego got in the way of creating a good film. "The way she treated him was appalling, and I know the director thought so too. There should have been the chemistry that Hank Fonda and Katy Hepburn had in *On Golden Pond*. But there was no chemistry. She just froze him out, and the film suffered."

Regular work in a weekly TV series was something Bette had seldom considered, favoring a variety of roles and avoiding being tied down to the routine and demands of series television. Though a number of her contemporaries - Jane Wyman and Lana Turner in *Falcon Crest*, Barbara Belle Geddes in *Dallas*, Barbara Stanwyck in *The Colbys*, and Ava Gardner in *Knots Landing* - were turning to series TV, she had good reason to reconsider.

When she was approached to star in a new series that would feature her, but carry an ensemble cast with a

An unforgettable story of love and devotion.

Right of Way

BETTE DAVIS and JAMES STEWART
in
RIGHT OF WAY

weekly collection of new guest stars, she felt she might get the best of both worlds - a steady income and a chance to work with a variety of actors in changing stories. However, her health would throw her a huge curveball.

After being diagnosed with breast cancer, Bette underwent a mastectomy on June 9, 1983. Recuperating at

The New York Hospital, things went from bad to worse when she suffered several strokes just nine days later. Initially, there was fear she might not survive. However, after she weathered that storm, her biggest fears were that she would be an invalid for the remainder of her life and would she never be able to work again.

Bette had recently completed filming the pilot telefilm for the new Aaron Spelling TV series *Hotel*. Intended to combine the glamour of *Dynasty* with the serialized and guest star format of *The Love Boat,* the initial pilot film would set the story in San Francisco at the fictional St. Gregory Hotel. With the series loosely based on Arthur Hailey's 1965 novel of the same name, which also had inspired the 1967 film, Bette would play the grand dame hotel owner with James Brolin as the hotel manager. Melvyn Douglas had played the owner in the original feature film.

Bette had intended to continue on in the role, appearing regularly in the series, but allowing the younger actors to reduce the load of work in a weekly television show. After the stroke, she initially hoped to recover in time to return. She had told Spelling that she expected to be able to be back on the set by January 1984. In the interim, the producer cast Anne Baxter as her character's sister-in-law, who was there to fill in for her. Bette said that during her convalescence, she continued to receive scripts for her expected return. "Mr. Spelling kept sending me scripts for my future episodes in *Hotel*, each worse than the last. In the first episode after my return, I was to cure Anne Baxter, who had taken my character's place in my absence, of drug addiction. In another, I was to be taken hostage by terrorists."

Bette said that even though the scripts were wretched she truly wanted to return; but she eventually felt the quality of the show wasn't there, and she wasn't even sure if the producers expected her to return. "Had a suitable script arrived, I would definitely have returned to the series. I waited for an announcement to be made that I would not be back. When none came, I begged Aaron Spelling to issue a statement that I was not returning. I felt this was only fair to those who would tune in week after week expecting to see me."

Bette got her wish, and Spelling stuck with Baxter as the hotel matriarch. "After appearing in the pilot, it was never the show I imagined it could be or would have been, I think, had I continued in it," she wrote in her book *This 'N That*.

In all likelihood, Spelling had no intention of bringing Bette back, and she would have been happy to have the steady paycheck and work. Quality scripts had not

always been that forthcoming in recent years and her track record was hit or miss. In fact, Bette appeared little in the pilot and came off far more frail and wooden than she would have liked. For her though, there was concern that if it had been announced that poor health prevented her from working it would have risked future offers. "Acting had been my life," she wrote. "I wouldn't want to live if I could never act again."

It would take years for Bette to recover, and in some ways, she never really did. She managed to get back to work, but her health would become a major factor in getting cast, and studio insurance companies would always be concerned that the star wouldn't survive her next job.

Wicked Stepmother would feel the burn of insurance challenges on every level. As Bette aged, the risks became even greater and insurance all the more important. For her final picture, if it hadn't been for the insurance, it's likely the film never would have been completed.

16

"*The Whales of August should have been her final film, even though Bette looked pretty bad in that one, too. She played a blind woman who was mostly confined to a chair, so she didn't have to walk around and do very much. The Whales of August was a quality picture, but I think Wicked Stepmother is far from the worst movie Bette ever made.*"

- Larry Cohen, Writer/Director of *Wicked Stepmother*

Chapter 16

A Whale of a Movie

D iagnosed with breast cancer, she had a mastectomy. It was just after completing the filming for the pilot to the TV series, **Hotel**. Bette bowed out of continuing with the series, handing things over to Anne Baxter, who ironically played the young ingénue out to replace her character in **All About Eve**. She originally hoped to get back to work, but nine days after her mastectomy she suffered a severe stroke. While recovering three months later, she fell and broke her hip. The surgery that followed made her recovery elusive. Frail, she weighed less than 90 pounds, but she was unwilling to give in to illness and disability. Bette fought back much to the amazement of her doctors. By 1987, she was well enough to undertake co-starring with Lillian Gish in **The Whales of August,** offering a harsh, but delicate portrayal of an aging blind woman facing death.

...

"I only got a ringside table at the Golden Globes because I showed up with my sister, Ronni Chasen, one of the industry's foremost publicists. When it was announced that Bette Davis would be presenting the next award, there was thunderous applause, which changed into waves of shock as she appeared on stage, dragging one withered leg behind her," recalled Larry Cohen. "Bette couldn't have weighed more than 80 pounds, and she was clearly recovering from a stroke."

Cohen said the evening stuck with him. Months later, he saw the star on a talk show and her condition had improved. "Perhaps she was making public appearances in

hopes that someone would take notice and offer her a job," Cohen thought.

Cohen then heard that Bette had been cast opposite Lillian Gish in *The Whales of August* and thought maybe her strategy had worked, but there was a little more to the story. It was actually back in the early 1980s that Bette Davis was originally offered a starring role in *The Whales of August*, a story of two elderly sisters living in a cottage along the coast of Maine. Davis's role was that of Libby, the blind and embittered older sister to Sarah, a good-natured caring sister. Davis turned down the role after learning that her younger sister would be played by Lillian Gish - a woman who was 14 years older than she.

At the time, Bette believed that better work was still out there for her, but after her close call with death, followed by a lengthy recovery, she realized that better work was not forthcoming. When the project was revived several years later and roles were harder to come by, Davis was more agreeable when approached to costar in the film.

Bette didn't really know Gish before filming began. She was certainly aware of her career, and that Gish had started out in the business long before she did. She met the actress once before. In February 1983, the two women shared a dressing room at Radio City Music Hall for the filming of *Night of a Hundred Stars*. In fact, they shared the dressing room with several other leading ladies, including Alice Faye, Joan Collins, June Allyson and Ginger Rogers. Bette recalled that she and Alice Faye seemed to have the most in common and found humor in watching Gish interact with Collins. "We were hysterical watching Lillian Gish, who is definitely from another world, looking at Joan Collins. Probably thinking, just bosoms and hair and no talent."

Several years later when the two were cast alongside each other, Gish remained composed, pleasant, and happy to be working alongside actors like Davis, Ann Southern, and Vincent Price. On the other hand, Bette was reportedly nasty throughout the production to Gish. According to those on the set, it was for no known reason other than a suspicion that Bette did not want to share the screen with anyone, especially not another screen legend.

Those who knew of Davis's antics on the set of *What Ever Happened to Baby Jane?,* and her treatment of costar

Joan Crawford, were not surprised. "Many attached to the production would claim that Bette took advantage of the fact that Gish's hearing was impaired, deliberately lowering her voice during their scenes so that Gish wouldn't be able to hear her cues," said her *Wicked Stepmother* director Larry Cohen. "Bette angrily responded to these rumors telling me, 'It's a total lie. Miss Gish was stone deaf. She couldn't have heard the cues if I'd shouted them through a bullhorn,'" he said.

Director of *The Whales of August,* Lindsay Anderson saw Bette's fierce determination up close. "Bette had battled her way back to work but the stroke's effect was still quite evident," said Anderson. "She was brave, eager to film and not at all passive … Bette was some 15 years younger than Lillian and inclined to be impatient. And I think it's no secret the lady is rather competitive."

After one scene, when the director complimented Gish after a lengthy close-up, telling her she photographed beautifully, Davis snapped back, "Well, she should! She was there when they invented close-ups."

After the movie was finished, the media gushed over Gish's magnificent performance. When buzz of an Oscar nomination for Gish began and not her, Davis refused to promote the film. It was a strong feature nonetheless, and a project of which Davis could be proud of.

"While Bette Davis has indeed always been one of my idols, she did make mincemeat out of poor Lillian Gish when they made *The Whales of August*," recalled former costar Helen Hayes. "Lillian swears she'll never act again. So, first she drove me from the screen, now she'd driven Lillian. She's making a clean sweep of everyone our age."

For Davis, acting was her life. The need and desire to continue working was never more apparent than in the twilight of a magnificent career. When there were few roles available for aging actresses, Davis's performances consisted of talk shows, press interviews, and acceptance speeches for numerous lifetime achievement awards. After disappointing losses of roles in *Driving Miss Daisy* and *Steel Magnolias*, she felt that she had become more of a legend and less of an actress. She resented actresses like Gish, Jessica Tandy, Sylvia Sidney, and others who were still considered actors worthy of choice parts.

Aside from dealing with an absence of good scripts, Bette was enraged when her daughter's tell-all book, *My Mother's Keeper*, portrayed her as an egomaniacal, ruthless, self-absorbed star, who tried to control and ruin her daughter's life, as well as the lives of B.D.'s husband, children, and Bette's own husbands.

Devastated that her own daughter would stoop to the same level as Joan Crawford's daughter to cash in on her notoriety, Bette was angry and bitter, calling the book, "a glaring lack of loyalty," and telling B.D. that she should rather be thankful, "for the very privileged life you have been given."

B.D. tried to explain the book, insisting that her story was not the same as Christina Crawford's. "Joan was completely evil," said B.D. "My mother is not, though she certainly has the capacity to be very mean when crossed."

Nothing helped mend the relationship, and Bette cut off contact with her daughter except to respond to her through her own book. Bette even reportedly stopped payment on a $500 check to pay for bicycles for B.D.'s two sons.

Bette decided to counter her daughter's accusations, or at least respond to them, by writing her own book. With help from her personal assistant Kathryn Sermak, she authored *This 'n That*, a book of anecdotes, recollections, and memories from her many years in show business.

Larry Cohen, still eager to work with one of the last remaining icons of Golden Hollywood, picked up a copy of Bette's book and took note. "While reading it, I got the idea for a Bette Davis movie," he said. "The horrendous condition she was in would work for this comedy about a happily married, young couple who return from a vacation to discover that the wife's widowed father had gotten married in their absence. My God, he's married Bette Davis, and she's already moved in – and even worse, she insists on being called 'Mom'!"

Cohen quickly began to build on his idea and a script quickly took shape. "I imagined having to live under the same roof with a vitriolic Bette Davis, and from there the screenplay wrote itself," he said. "Within a week I had finished the script for *Wicked Stepmother,* which I promptly sent to Bette's agent. It was instantly rejected. I later learned that Bette had never even seen it. Knowing my previous credits, her agents had assumed *Wicked Stepmother* was a horror movie and passed on it, unread."

However, Larry Cohen was not one to give up easily.

17

"Unfortunately, she didn't always tell it the way it is. She misled me into thinking she could do the part when she knew that she couldn't. She tried to get through it and then, when that proved impossible, she tried to get out of it by blaming me in public."

- Larry Cohen, Writer/Director of *Wicked Stepmother*

Chapter 17

Return to Being Wicked

Nestled between North Hollywood and Mid-Wilshire, Hancock Park is a quiet, tree-lined neighborhood in the heart of Los Angeles. With large single-family homes, well-manicured lawns and quick access to major thoroughfares like North Highland Avenue and Interstate 10, it was a good nearby location for local Hollywood filming. Bette Davis, in fact, was quite familiar with Hancock Park. In 1962, she joined Joan Crawford, Victor Bueno, Anna Lee, and her daughter B.D. to film Robert Aldrich's **What Ever Happened to Baby Jane?** at a mansion in Hancock Park. When Larry Cohen scouted locations for his Bette Davis black comedy, another Hancock Park mansion, blocks away from Aldrich's location, was ideal for the family home. The house even featured a guesthouse in back that he could use for his star when she wasn't shooting.

...

"I couldn't give up, however, since there was no one else who could play the part," recalled Larry Cohen, after the initial rejection of his script for *Wicked Stepmother*.

Cohen said that months later his publicist, Milt Kahn, casually mentioned that he knew actor, author, and film historian Robert Osborne, and Osborne just happened to be a friend of Bette Davis. More than that, Osborne actually lived in the same apartment building as the elusive star. It was through Osborne, with help from Kahn, that Cohen was able to get his script into the hands of Bette. Osborne didn't read the script - had he, he may never have agreed to pass it on. "I always felt that Bette Davis was one of the great screen actresses who never really got her due -

she won two Oscars, but the last was in 1938, and that was really before all the great work that she did," said Osborne." Cohen was grateful that he did hand her his script and hoped the star would at least look it over this time. "Bette called just a few days later. I knew it was her because there was smoke coming out of the telephone," joked Cohen. "Her voice crackled over the line like sparks from a frayed old electrical cord. 'Well, I certainly got a few laughs thanks to you last night,' she snapped. 'Am I mistaken or did you

write this especially for me?'" said Cohen, telling her indeed he had.

Her agent's professional recommendation was that Bette turn down the project. However, eager to work, Bette tried to look past the script's flaws and saw the laughs and potential. On the phone with Cohen, she agreed to consider the project, and the two arranged to meet at her home. "She was clearly flattered and was interested in meeting me personally. Would I drop by her place on Havenhurst for a cocktail? Naturally I jumped at the opportunity and brought along my agent, Peter Sabiston," Cohen recalled later.

Bette had downsized from the palatial Hollywood homes of her golden years, when marriages, children and fame required her to live a large life in movie star mansions. Back in the late 70s, when she was looking for a place to live in Los Angeles, Roddy McDowell called her and told her he'd found her a place. He was investing in real estate and suggested a condo development. She knew the area, having lived next door with her first husband years ago.

Instead of staying in hotels when she was in Los Angeles, Bette had decided to leave the east coast and head back to Hollywood permanently. She purchased a pristine, two-bedroom condo for $125,000, saying, "This is my last home! They can just carry me out the door when it's over and take me over to Forest Lawn, where, if I wasn't dead already, I'd die from the fumes of the freeway below!"

With age and health troubles limiting her mobility, life set on one floor was more suitable, and the renovated space was well apportioned. Still, the smaller scale made life easier. Her condo was just off Sunset Boulevard, but it was a nice sized space in a comfortable and private, gated complex. Built just before World War II, the place had been completely remodeled before Bette moved in. It wasn't showy or garish, noted Cohen when he arrived. "Contrary to expectations, there was no memorabilia of her career visible. No posters, no photos with celebrities, and no trace of the two Oscars she'd won," recalled Cohen after his arrival.

Though he saw little signs of the star of years gone by, Cohen did see one sign of her glorious past. "On one wall I did notice a tiny charcoal sketch of a person most wouldn't recognize. It was George Arliss, the noted stage star, who'd made films for Warner Bros. in the Thirties," said Cohen. "He had actually discovered Bette and insisted she appear in his movie *The Man Who Played God*. Jack Warner had intended to drop her contract at that time and it was only through Arliss's intervention that the studio relented. Within a few years, Davis would be the highest-salaried woman in America. She had never forgotten what Arliss had done for her."

Joining Bette at their initial meeting that day was her assistant, Kathryn Sermak. Sermak had worked for Davis on and off since 1979 and had become her friend as much as a secretary and personal assistant. "Kathryn had become virtually a surrogate daughter to Bette and would someday inherit half of her estate," said Cohen.

The director was surprised to see several photos of her daughter B.D. Hyman prominently displayed, despite the fact that the two were not on speaking terms at the time. "Taking notice of my interest in the photos, she quickly commented, 'If your children like you, you can't have been a very good mother,'" noted Cohen.

Bette was agreeable and interested in the film offer. Against the advice of her agent, she wanted the work. "There was no question that Bette loved my script and wanted to do it," said Cohen.

However, Cohen had his own reservations about whether she was up to the task. Considering that Bette weighed likely no more than 90 pounds and was still a bit unsure on her feet, he had to wonder if her health would prevent her from completing the film. Frail and limping after years of health troubles including a broken hip, Davis was a far cry from the vibrant young woman who found fame in the movies. She was even a distant memory of the figure that she carved from the countless horror films in which she starred in over the previous two decades. "As soon as we'd left her apartment, Pete pulled me aside saying, 'How can you even consider making a movie with a woman in her condition?'" Cohen recalled.

Cohen knew that he would have trouble insuring the completion of the picture, but he believed her talent, wit, and personality were intact and proceeded to move forward. If he could get the financing, the rest would take care of itself, he thought.

He also believed that her name still had some marketability. "I knew it was foolhardy, but I just couldn't let it go. After all, she would be playing a witch - a particularly appropriate role for a woman who had often been accused of being one - or something that sounded quite similar," Cohen noted.

Davis never doubted her own abilities and believed the script had enough laughs, special effects and twists to succeed at the box office. She was on board, but hoped the picture would show that she still had fans who would pay to see her on the screen. "In a long career, sometimes you find yourself competing with your own past," she admitted.

Cohen said during the preliminary planning of the film she visited his home near Coldwater Canyon. She dropped by occasionally to discuss the script, he said, and he soon came to realize that she had a strong addiction to cigarettes. While he knew that she used them as a prop in her films, he didn't know how heavy a smoker she was until he started working with her. "And I have the cigarette burn marks on the furniture to prove it," he laughed.

"Bette couldn't have been more affectionate as she walked us to the door that first day. But soon, difficulties arose when her attorney and longtime manager, Harold Schiff, decided he wasn't sure if he wanted Bette to appear in a Larry Cohen movie," said Cohen. "I had no choice but to fly to New York and try to convince Schiff to change his opinion. I must've charmed the hell out of him, because he completely reversed himself, and we quickly closed a deal for Bette."

Cohen had a binding commitment to pay Bette a quarter of a million dollars, but had no studio to finance the picture. "I enlisted my pal, Robert Littman, to join me as producer. Bobby had important connections, one of which paid off. Alan Ladd Jr., who then headed MGM, agreed to finance our picture to the tune of $2.5 million," said Cohen.

At a salary of $250,000, Bette Davis agreed to star in *Wicked Stepmother*. Due to her age and poor health, producers of the MGM-financed picture were required to insure the film to the tune of $1 million in the event health problems or death of the star caused the film to go unfinished. Davis was then required to undergo a health examination before the insurance company would write up the policy. Davis passed the test, but it later appeared that she intimidated the doctor who examined her, and the exam did not even capture the most standard piece of information – her weight.

Cohen would say that pre-production with Bette was a challenge at best. He said it was "consistently amusing,"

but at the same time, felt that she was in such dire need of attention that it became exhausting. "She got into the habit of phoning me day or night with any thoughts that she might have at the moment, quickly stating an opinion then hanging up without even saying goodbye," Cohen said. "For example, I'd pick up the phone and hear that unmistakable rasp, 'Larry, I've decided that my character must have red hair rather than my normal color.' Click. And she'd be gone."

Even so, he had aligned the stars and managed to get his production afloat. He lined up David Rasche to play Bette's son-in-law and Colleen Camp as her stepdaughter. Though only in her 30s, Camp had been around Hollywood for years, landing small and supporting roles in films like *Funny Lady, Smile, Game of Death, Apocalypse Now, Clue, They All Laughed* ,and *Valley Girl*. *Wicked Stepmother* was another supporting role, but also a chance to work with a legend like Bette Davis.

Rasche, on the other hand, had first appeared on film in 1978 in Paul Mazursky's film *An Unmarried Woman* and shortly after in a small part in Woody Allen's *Manhattan*. While his film career didn't lead to starring roles, he found more success on television - carving out two seasons on the TV series *Sledgehammer* and other notable appearances on hit shows like *Miami Vice, Kate and Allie, LA*

Law, Empty Nest, Columbo, and more. *Wicked Stepmother* would mark one of his more substantial roles on feature film.

For the role of her new husband, Lionel Stander was cast. Stander's career dated back as far as Bette's. Born in 1908 a few months before Bette, Stander began his film career in the early 1930s and continued with more recent work in the popular TV series, *Hart to Hart,* which subsequently spawned a series of telefilms that kept the actor busy. He even worked with Joan Crawford in *The Ice Follies of 1939.*

For the role of Priscilla, Bette's daughter in the film, Cohen tested actress Laurene Landon. Landon had worked with Cohen before and was familiar with his style.

However, Cohen didn't feel she had the right demeanor to play the devilish character and offered the part to Barbara Carrera instead. Landon would go on to play a smaller role in the film, as a woman working on a game show, similar to *Wheel of Fortune's* Vanna White. Landon recalled her screen test, acting opposite the Hollywood legend. "She appeared very ill and frail. After I was done reading with her she said out loud, 'You are not bad. Actually, you are one hell of an actress. I am very, very impressed!' I ended up playing another part in the film because the producers decided I didn't look like a 'Witch.' They hired Barbara Carrera instead for that role."

Tom Bosley, Richard Moll, and Evelyn Keyes were other capable actors whom Cohen cast in his project. Bosley, ironically, had also appeared alongside Joan Crawford in one of her final roles - an appearance on *The Night Gallery*. This time, Davis would be his costar.

Now, all Cohen needed to do was to get it captured on film. Apparently, that feat would be easier said than done.

18

"Whenever a plane flew over the house while we were filming, ruining the take, Bette murmured, 'George Brent.' I asked her what she meant, and she explained that Brent (who had been her lover in real life and leading man in so many films) had his own plane and enjoyed flying. When Jack Warner suspended him and barred him from the lot, Brent simply piloted his private aircraft low over the studio soundstage in Burbank, circling endlessly. No one could shoot sound while Brent continued his harassment, and he was quickly rehired at full salary. Thereafter, every time a plane passed over our location I would shout 'George Brent' and Bette would crack up."

- Larry Cohen, Writer/Director of *Wicked Stepmother*

Chapter 18

A Wicked Exit

Bette Davis ultimately was called to appear in court to testify under oath on her exit from **Wicked Stepmother**. The insurance company, according to Writer/Director Larry Cohen, looked to "accurately assign blame for the shutdown and delay of the film."

Cohen said that he was happy with the outcome of the deposition. "And to her credit, she finally owned up to the truth and completely absolved me of any responsibility for her premature departure," he said.

However, the insurance company ultimately had to deliver a million dollars due to Davis's absence, and when the leading lady died roughly eight months after the film's release in 1989, **Wicked Stepmother** would become her final screen credit. Without the insurance payout, the film never would have been completed.

...

"It wasn't until Bette finally reported for work on a full-time basis that I realized the extent of her cigarette addiction," Larry Cohen remarked. "She smoked 100 Vantages every day. Before she arrived, five packs would be broken open and their contents placed in cups. Wherever

she went, Kathryn would follow Bette around with this supply of cigarettes. She was never without one. I suppose it took a lot of nerve to point out that all this smoking was bad for her. She replied, 'Oh, Larry, I know. But if I didn't have a cigarette in my hand I wouldn't know what to do with myself.'"

Pre-production began in the early months of 1988, with filming due to begin on April 4, a day before the star's 80th birthday. Initial work began with costume fittings for the star at a common Hollywood locale called Western Costume. "She had all their employees terrorized," claimed Cohen, when he arrived with Bette that afternoon. Cohen gave the actress control over her own wardrobe for the picture, but agreed to oversee her selections. According to Cohen, Davis asked the director to attend a fitting session to offer his opinion on her decisions. As he sat there she modeled the numerous outfits that she had selected for her character. "Everything was black," he said. When she asked him what he thought, he suggested that she add a splash of color here and there, using some sashes or handkerchiefs, because he felt everything looked too much alike. She immediately became upset, suggesting they toss it all out and start again. Cohen said that it would not be necessary and that some well-placed accessories would add a pop of color and splash where needed. She began to argue with him as costume fitters and assistants cowered outside the dressing room; but he stood firm, and she eventually agreed that the clothes would do.

Costume fitters were not the only ones frightened by the 90-pound powerhouse. Cinematographer Daniel Pearl met with Davis prior to filming and was told by the star that if she did not like the way he captured her on film, she would see to it that he was fired. Pearl called Cohen after the meeting. Fearing that the actress hated him, he was ready to bow out of the project, but Cohen persuaded him to hold off, so that he could to talk to the star to get her take on the meeting. Davis supposedly told Cohen she liked Pearl. The cinematographer then agreed to stay on and Davis began rehearsing her lines and scenes along with other members of the cast at Cohen's home that spring.

"We then relaxed together as she generously regaled us with tales of her career, particularly at Warners," recalled Cohen. "How Errol Flynn's trailer would rock visibly back and forth as he entertained young starlets between setups." Cohen laughed when Davis told him that none of the actresses at Warner Bros wanted to do love scenes with Edward G. Robinson. "He had those awful purple lips," Bette said. "She complained she never got to play opposite most of the great male stars. Jack Warner knew it wasn't necessary to pay top dollar for a male lead when Bette could carry a movie on her own," said Cohen.

Cohen's feature was a spoof of sorts of Davis's forays into horror, which included *Whatever Happened to Baby Jane; Hush ... Hush, Sweet Charlotte; Dead Ringer; Burnt Offerings,* and more. Principal photography on the black comedy was delayed from its intended April 4 start and actually began on April 25, with location filming set in Los Angeles. Much of the filming was done in a large home in luxurious Hancock Park. The local production would be far easier on Davis than lengthy, far-reaching location shooting for which many Hollywood films are known for.

In addition to Davis, Lionel Stander, Colleen Camp, and David Rasche were scheduled for the initial scenes. Other stars featured would include Tom Bosley as a police detective, and Barbara Carrera as Bette's daughter/

replacement, Priscilla, but those scenes would be filmed later since they didn't involve Bette. The story follows a witch named Miranda, played by Davis, who marries older men, helps get them rich, and then disposes of them – usually by shrinking them and putting them in a shoe box – moving onto the next husband and victim.

Even though MGM financed the production on a low budget, Cohen saw to it that Davis's dressing room on the set was luxurious, replete with a small kitchen with a microwave, and a sitting room with a TV and VCR. It was even reported that Cohen offered to have a bed installed in her trailer, should the star need some rest. "I've never lain down between takes," Davis bellowed back, refusing the offer. For the location work, a guesthouse behind the main house served as a private space for the star as well.

With the star still frail and limping, the director made adjustments to the script to accommodate her movements. The main change was in rewriting much of the action to minimize Davis's need for walking. This accommodation allowed the actress to deliver her lines with the action and other actors moving around her. She could perform with hand gestures and her standard cigarette prop while the camera moved instead of her. Even with attempts to put the star at ease, Davis found one aspect of production particularly troublesome. "He never rehearses actors," complained the actress. "He just rehearses the camera. So we work for the camera."

Ironically, Cohen's attempts to reduce Bette's need to move also made her uncomfortable due to the action swirling around her. "There was always a dolly running around!" she complained.

Even so, Davis refused to admit that she required any special treatment. In one instance, costar Colleen Camp reportedly offered to get a chair for the actress to sit in between takes. "If I want a chair, I'll get it," was Bette's

reply. "I was just trying to be nice," said Camp. "But then I realized this was her way of preserving her dignity."

During production, Davis was known for appearing on the set long before her scenes and would often stand directly in the middle of the set as the crew moved around her setting up the scenes. Cohen felt that it was her way of soaking up the atmosphere of filmmaking. "The men would walk around her and say, 'Excuse me, Miss Davis,' and barely miss her head with a ladder or cable," explained Cohen. He would ask her what she was doing in the middle

of the set, and she would tell him that she liked to see what was going on, or that she did not like being in her dressing room.

Even though Bette enjoyed the experience of being on the set, she wasn't always the warmest costar, as many actors who worked with her would testify. However, the chance to work with a Hollywood legend was hard to pass up. "Colleen [Camp] and David [Rasche] wanted to be in the picture, because Bette was going to be in it," said Cohen. "Let's not forget, whatever state Bette was in, she was still Hollywood royalty. I'm sure they both enjoyed meeting Bette and hanging out with her, although I don't think Bette really had much to do with anybody on the movie except me. She wasn't unfriendly to anybody, but she did spend a little time in her dressing room. If anybody brought friends or relatives to the set to meet her, Bette was

always cordial and pleasant. She would sit down with any visitors, chat with them, and exchange anecdotes. I wouldn't say that Bette was aloof with the cast members, but she wasn't that chummy with them either."

Even so, costar Lionel Stander enjoyed appearing as the screen legend's husband. "In *Wicked Stepmother* Bette Davis does me the honor of hypnotizing me in marriage," he explained. "I'm a man of means, my daughter's away, Miranda [Davis] has magic powers, my daughter comes home, boom, Miranda's running things."

No sooner had the first full week of production began when trouble started brewing. One major mishap came in the form of a dangerous special effect. Davis was supposed to put a cigarette in her mouth that would immediately light up without the need for a match. The scene could have been done with optical effects, but to keep expenses down, a sparking device was devised to make the cigarette light up with the cameras rolling. In the first take, the cigarette flared up, coming very close to burning Bette's face. Cohen claimed that after that scare, he told the star that they would use the optical effect rather than risk harming her. However, the actress refused and demanded they try another take. Two more takes followed, and each time the prop flared up. The footage did manage to make its way, briefly, into the final cut.

Cohen recalled the scene years later this way. "We tried a third take, during which the cigarette ignited with incendiary force. There was a flash of fire, and Bette was clasping both hands over her right eye, which apparently had been scorched. The effects artist was instantly banished from the set. Minutes later, Bette recovered, never complaining about any further discomfort. But I was to hear more of this later."

Bette later claimed that improper planning and lack of rehearsal would lead to many of the problems during production. "I was very uncomfortable in all the scenes he had me play in that week, because he worried about the camera."

The star's determination to convince cast and crew that she needed no special treatment on the set took a troubled turn during that week of filming. Davis took a fall while walking across the set one afternoon, but no one came to her aid. Some reports claim that due to her numerous refusals of help, the director had urged the cast and crew to let Davis manage on her own. The 80-year-old

actress struggled for some time trying to get back on her feet, but to no avail. Colleen Camp believed that the actress struggled for about five minutes, but Cohen claimed it was longer and may have been as long as 20 minutes.

The story goes that eventually, a couple of crew members helped her by placing several wooden crates beside the struggling star so that she could use them to get back up on her own. Bruised from the fall, she limped back to her trailer, but then returned to work a short time later, refusing to take any time off to recuperate from her spill. "I remained out of sight–or so I thought," recalled Cohen. "Bette had an eagle eye. Somehow, she had caught a glimpse of me; and when I finally came to her dressing room to offer sympathy, she let me know she'd seen me "hiding" when she was in distress. I explained that I'd tried to spare her any extra embarrassment, and she finally agreed that had been the best approach."

During an evening shoot, another problem arose, recalled Cohen. "While we were trying to film in Hancock Park, the teenagers next door deliberately turned up their stereo so as to harass us. It would be impossible to record sound with all that racket coming from next door."

Cohen was about to deal with the situation when Bette approached him and asked, "Want me to go over and tell them to turn it off?"

Cohen chuckled inside at the thought of these young kids opening their front door to see Bette Davis demanding they shut off their boom box. "I thanked her, but chose to send a production assistant over with a crisp $100 bill. The music soon stopped. But I was amused at Bette's willingness to pitch in."

As the first week of filming charged on, another problem became apparent and couldn't be overcome with a $100 bill. Bette's cracked denture began slipping, making it difficult for Davis to deliver her lines. Initially, it wasn't apparent that there was a problem, and Cohen said that no one, except Davis herself, could tell that her dentures were slipping. But Cohen explained that the star began taking awkward pauses between her lines due to the issue, and later edited out as many of the pauses as he could.

However, when Davis saw the initial rushes of her raw footage, she was not happy, and said that she no longer had complete trust in her director to do right by her, no matter what he told her. She was also unhappy, because she didn't feel that her director was interested in her opinion. "If he had gone in and seen the rushes daily he would have seen that there was a problem dentally," she said. "But he never does. On the screen I looked uncomfortable. And I was."

According to Cohen, Bette began begging him to see the dailies. He said he resisted over several days until, "one afternoon she beckoned me into an empty room in the house and burst into tears. I couldn't believe Bette Davis was crying.

Maybe this was just another tactic, but I couldn't resist. I agreed to have dailies shown to her on Saturday."

Bette confirmed the story. "Before I left, I told him I had to see the rushes film footage from the first week's work. I've always tried to be very very honest with audiences ... I was very upset with these rushes."

Filming continued during the first week of May with Bette appearing for some location shooting at the house in Hancock Park. For the star, the situation didn't improve; and it was reported that on Friday night May 6 - roughly two weeks into the production - Davis flew from Los Angeles to New York to see her dentist. The director reported that her departure was amicable and that she even gave him a kiss goodbye. "Each day at the conclusion of her last scene, Bette would pooch out her lips in my direction, demanding our traditional goodbye kiss," recalled Cohen. "Sometimes the AD would tell me that she'd signed out but had waited a full 20 minutes before leaving because she had to personally say goodnight. She did so on her very last day of production. I had no idea she'd never be coming back."

The dental issue was apparently more serious than first suspected, requiring Davis to undergo surgery and extensive dental work to repair her bridge. The medical procedures took its toll on the feisty star. She lost considerable weight - dropping as much as 13 pounds, down from 88 pounds to a mere 75 pounds.

The media initially reported that the star would return to the picture. Cohen busied himself and kept the production afloat for the first few weeks of her absence by shooting around her. He then suspended production for two weeks, as speculation and rumors began to whirl about whether or not his star would return.

In late May, it was reported that Davis would indeed return to the devilish role. Costar Barbara Carrera, who actually began work on the film the day after Davis left for New York, told reporters, "We've been informed that Miss Davis is coming back and that there was a medical problem

with her jaw that has been taken care of and that production will resume the end of the month."

Production had to begin again soon, with or without Davis; because Carrera was committed to another film,

Loverboy, which was also already in production, with her scenes scheduled for shooting at the end of May.

"It's basically been a health problem," agreed Cohen, adding, "If you're not feeling well, and things are bothering you, like dental problems, it's hard to work. Now that's been taken care of, she's coming back."

However, shortly after giving the statement to the press, Cohen received word that Davis would be unable to return anytime soon. Her business manager then called and raised objections to numerous aspects of the production. It became clear that the star would not be returning. Cohen suspected that her health problems were the cause, telling reporters that it was mutually agreed that the star would depart the production. It was also suspected that the actress was already concerned about her appearance on film and that the weight loss from her illness only exacerbated her concerns. Bette told Nina Easton of the *Los Angeles Times* that, "[I]t could seriously be the end of anybody ever hiring me again."

Cohen was initially as perplexed as anyone as to Davis's exit. He simply moved on with his film without her and put all his options on the table. "There was never much published about Bette's dental problems, because I chose not to respond in public to any of her remarks or those made by other people. I didn't want to attack Bette or do anything that might prevent her from making another movie. Perhaps, somebody else would have hired Bette after her teeth were fixed, and I didn't want to say anything bad," said Cohen.

By the time Bette finally bowed out, Cohen wasn't surprised and Cohen had already been weighing various options on how to handle her exit. "I liked Bette, and even our last conversation on the phone before she left, was very friendly," he said. "She actually apologized and never accused me of anything. She said, 'Larry, I've made a terrible mistake, and I can't continue.' If only she had come to me before and told me about them. I would not have fired her. I would have listened and tried to find a resolution to this situation that satisfied everybody. That would have been better than Bette basically trying to deceive me."

Cohen, however, felt she left him in a difficult spot, and it was one that could have been avoided. "Unfortunately, she didn't always tell it the way it is. She misled me into thinking she could do the part when she knew that she couldn't. She tried to get through it and then, when that proved impossible, she tried to get out of it by blaming me in public. Of course, some journalists knew the facts and reported her version, as well as the truth. I just kept my mouth shut."

19

"At this point, I had no choice but to pull the plug. There was an effort to hire Lucille Ball as a replacement, but we found that Lucy was in the hospital herself, and near death."

- Larry Cohen, Writer/Director of *Wicked Stepmother*

Chapter 19

Here's Lucy?

W hen Lucille Ball was just 15, she convinced her mother to enroll her in the New York City drama school conducted by John Murray Anderson and Robert Milton. Alongside her in class was another youngster named Bette Davis. "I was a tongue-tied teenager spellbound by the school's star pupil - Bette Davis," Ball recalled. Lucy was apparently so tongue-tied that the school was unconvinced she even belonged there. The school wrote to her mother, saying "Lucy's wasting her time and ours. She's too shy and reticent to put her best foot forward."

Lucy, however, persevered and gained her footing and began projecting in class and taking an active role. After completing her education, Ball pounded the New York streets, landing first job in 1927. While it was only a small part in a third road company of the musical comedy *Rio Rita,* Ball was *on her way. In time she became be one of the most successful comedians in the business.*

*Years later, when Ball was starring in her sitcom **I Love Lucy,** she and husband Desi Arnaz had an episode where Lucy meets a celebrity living next door. Lucy had Bette Davis in mind as the star and Davis agreed to appear if she were paid $20,000 - the same amount Lucy and Desi were making for each episode as stars of series. Davis also wanted her airfare to fly to and from Hollywood covered as well. While Bette's demands were exorbitant, they agreed. However, Davis fell off a horse, cracking her vertebra and had to cancel the appearance. Lucy hired Tallulah Bankhead to replace her, much to Bette's disappointment.*

...

By June, Larry Cohen was still working to keep his film afloat, even though his star was missing. He'd been shooting scenes not involving Davis and working around her absence while she was in New York, initially hoping she'd return. It wasn't until he received a note from Bette's dentist on June 1 that indicated things were worse than Cohen expected. "Ms. Davis has lost approximately 15 pounds and now weighs 75 pounds and is therefore exhausted," said the message, implying it would be impossible for the star to muster the strength to return to the picture.

Davis herself had given Cohen fair warning that the scenario was bleak. "I'd spoken to her briefly when she called me to say she wasn't coming back," recalled Cohen.

"I made a terrible mistake, Larry," said Davis. "I have to leave the picture."

As Davis's departure from the film became imminent, Cohen said she sounded terribly sad, "On the edge of being apologetic," and that he didn't attempt to change her mind. "I simply wished her well."

After the fateful call, the director spent a week negotiating with Bette's lawyers, though he still held out hope she might find the strength to return. Since Davis had worked for only one week of the intended five-week shoot, it was agreed that she'd receive one-fifth of her agreed salary - $50,000. For Cohen this meant the remaining $200,000 could be put back into the production, helping cover special effects costs as he reworked the script.

To get the production made in the first place, Cohen had to insure the picture to the tune of $2.5 million in the event that the film could not be completed. While any number of circumstances can cause the demise of a film,

Davis' age and frailty added concerns that she would either die or be unable to finish her work due to ill health.

With Davis out, decisions had to be made on what to do. If production folded, the insurance company was on the hook to pay up to $2.5 million to cover the contracts and fees owed to cast and crew. The only alternative was to finish the picture.

Cohen really only had three options. First, he could look to hold the project in the hopes that Davis would recover and resume work on the film. "Recalling how she'd walked off the set of *The Little Foxes* after a dispute with

William Wyler, but had dutifully returned nearly a month later, I thought surely I'd get her back," thought Cohen at the time.

However, the scenario of her return was looking less and less likely each day. Option number two was to recast the star of his picture and re-film the scenes Bette completed. Finding someone other than Bette Davis who could pull it off was the key. Cohen thought one other actress might make a suitable replacement - Lucille Ball.

An unlikely choice, Lucille Ball would present the best alternative to Bette Davis. With her trademark red hair, build, age, and demeanor, she'd bring a broader level of comedy to the film, as opposed to Davis's more traditional Grand Guignol approach. Ball also had the face and name that would provide an equal audience draw to that of Davis.

Ball's last big screen appearance was in 1974's *Mame*. While she had a formidable career in the movies dating back to the mid-1930s, her greatest fame came in television with decades of success starring in shows like *I Love Lucy, The Lucy Show, Here's Lucy,* and her most recent series, *Life*

With Lucy, which was cancelled after only 13 episodes in 1986. With dismal ratings, the network only aired eight episodes and never scheduled the remaining five.

With five Emmys and a host of other awards, Ball recently showed more depth at the dramatic in the 1985 TV movie *Stone Pillow*. However, like Davis, as the years passed, work was harder to obtain than lifetime achievement awards.

Unfortunately, Ball was in even worse health than Bette when it came to starring in a feature film. In 1987 she was hospitalized to have a cyst removed from her thyroid gland and was suffering from cardiac problems that resulted in more hospital stays in 1988. in early April 1989, Ball was diagnosed with a dissecting aortic aneurysm and underwent a 7-hour surgery to repair her aorta and successfully install an aortic valve replacement, but her health never improved. Lucille Ball died at the age of 77 on April 26, 1989, six months before Davis.

Cohen was out of luck and had to think quickly before things were shut down for good. Though he initially hoped that there were an outside chance Davis might change her mind, as June progressed it became clear that there was no chance of that possibility.

The decision to shut down the production was a tough one. His chance of working with a Hollywood legend would be behind him, and a large group of people would lose work and paychecks if the production were cancelled. "At this point, I had no choice but to pull the plug. There was an effort to hire Lucille Ball as a replacement. But we found that Lucy was in the hospital herself, and near death."

However, there was a third option. Cohen believed that there was still a chance he could complete the picture with Davis as the name on the marque. He approached MGM and made his case for reworking the script without her. "I argued that with Bette the picture would have a life on video, television, and cable. I would salvage the footage she'd shot and rewrite the script to accommodate her disappearance," said Cohen. "Fortunately, Bette played a witch, so she could transform herself into a beautiful young woman at will. Barbara Carrera appeared in the film as Bette's daughter, but I'd switch it, so she'd play the ravishing creature that Bette becomes. Everything else in the script could remain the same. We'd be back in production in 10 days."

Cohen had already invested considerable time and film in Davis. Her name was one of the key selling points for making the film initially. He decided to continue the film with her as its star by rewriting the script without Davis's Miranda.

The feeble attempt took its toll on the production and much of what might have made the film worthwhile was lost in the rewrite. "The original script was very funny," claimed costar Colleen Camp. "It was disheartening for Larry to try to rewrite it. It didn't make the sense it made originally."

However, rewrite it he did. Cohen's initial plan was for Davis to change a black cat in the film into the beautiful Carrera and pass her off as her daughter. The rewrite had Davis transforming herself into Carrera, showing up on the doorstep claiming to be the star's daughter. Thus, he never had to actually film a scene with the two actresses together, yet kept the story going. Davis had filmed enough footage before her departure to keep her in the first third of the picture. However, serious editing, dubbing and other effects would have to be used to keep her spirit alive throughout the film, including a cigarette-smoking cat and a bizarre exorcism-like scene at the end of the movie. Carrera also had to film a number of scenes that were originally planned for Davis.

"I always admired Bette Davis. She made such wonderful roles - so varied," said Carrera. "How could I imagine I would inherit Bette Davis's final role, to actually play her part? But the movies are magic, and that movie is a fairly tale!"

According to *Wicked Stepmother* co-star Colleen Camp, after Bette walked off the production, Cohen briefly considered Bea Arthur as a possible star. Cohen said he also

thought about Carol Burnett as a possible substitute; however, before recasting the role, he decided a rewrite of the story was the more economical way to go. His solution to turn Davis into a much younger seductress with Barbara Carrera in the role would save money by not having to hire another star and optimizing getting Bette Davis for only $50,000.

Cohen then gave the bulk of Davis's dialog for the remainder of the film to Carrera. Carrera had already been cast in the film, but had yet to appear on set, so she never worked with Davis. Cohen decided to jettison the un-filmed scenes of them together and adjust his story to make them one character rather than two.

Since Bette had left Cohen with roughly 20 minutes of usable footage for the film he decided to use special effects to try and keep her character alive. He hired actor and female impersonator Michael Greer to dub in some of the star's dialog. Few would notice. Cohen just wanted to find his way through what had become a very challenging picture. When Davis was contacted about the film being completed using footage she'd already filmed, her response was simply, "No comment. I absolutely will never comment on this film."

"I myself would have been paid my entire fee so I had nothing to gain financially," said Cohen. "I simply wanted to salvage what I was certain would be Bette's last screen appearance, and to save everyone concerned from financial disaster. I was trying to create order out of chaos."

20

"*I hate to say it, but the best parts of* **Wicked Stepmother** *are those in which Bette Davis does not appear. The rest of the cast was excellent. But when Bette comes on screen, her physical condition is so shocking that the audience is in no mood to laugh. Still, it would have been a shame to toss her final performance in the scrap heap.*"

- Larry Cohen, Writer/Director of *Wicked Stepmother*

Chapter 20

Stepmother Comes and Bette Goes

Writer and director of **Wicked Stepmother**, Larry Cohen was in Tanzania on a safari when he heard news on the radio that Bette Davis had died in a Paris hospital. He said that her cancer must have been undiagnosed and advanced by the time she began working with him. "It later became clear that when she took the medical exam as required before appearing in any movie, she'd so bamboozled the doctor that he never actually touched her."

On the day of Davis's memorial, Cohen said that he had paid tribute of his own by spending the afternoon "watching Bette Davis movies and wishing that I'd known her in her prime and had the opportunity to direct her when she was still in possession of all her faculties."

However, Cohen admitted that Davis would likely never have agreed to work with him or in one of his films during her

peak. "It was a trade-off and I suppose I still got the best of the
bargain."

...

Initially, Davis did not believe she'd be featured in Cohen's film, believing that there wasn't enough usable footage of her – and certainly not enough to make her the star of the picture. One theory was that she believed the film would be scrapped.

However, when it became apparent that scenario was not the case, Davis took to bad-mouthing the picture and trying to discredit the director in an effort to protect her own career. "I think that for the good of my future career, I honestly had no choice but to go public with the story," said Davis, as she detailed her version of the troubled production.

Davis contended that Cohen refused to listen to her advice, and she criticized his directorial style. "I was perfectly able, had the conditions been right, to return to the film," claimed the star.

After seeing the dailies before exiting the picture, she told the press she felt that Cohen had deceived her. "Many of the scenes I wasn't in had nothing to do with the script I had approved. Much of that week's work had, well, to me, many vulgar moments."

The star said she had agonized over the issue of returning to the film, eventually concluding that she had no choice but not to return because she felt, "nothing would change."

One scene in particular that upset Davis was the inside gag that later provided one of the few genuine laughs in the entire picture. In the scene, Davis's stepdaughter, played by Camp, glimpses at the photo of her natural mother recalling how kind and wonderful she was. The photo was an image of Davis's longtime Hollywood nemesis known for her infamous mothering skills – Joan Crawford. Davis said the scene was "in terrible taste," but the director refused to cut the scene. "The lesser of the two evils was my courage in not returning," Bette told one interviewer about bowing out of the film.

Thanks to a million dollar payout from the insurance policy on Davis, the production had the funds to continue and by mid-August, the film was basically finished. The footage was shot, and with later editing and effects, Cohen crafted it into a full motion picture, but the question was – would the studio and the public buy it? "I'm not certain this type of solution has ever been effected before," said Cohen at the time. "But then, not too many films have been done about witches."

While Cohen continued to explain that health reasons were the only cause for Davis's departure, he did take the opportunity to deliver at least one dig at the star when it was reported that he took a stab in the dark, guessing that the several packs of cigarettes Davis smoked every day didn't do much for improving her health.

In the finished movie, the first nine minutes feature actor Tom Bosley investigating a missing family who have been swindled out of their life savings by an old woman. We get a first glimpse of Bette about 10 minutes in. Davis then appears on screen for roughly the next 12 minutes, followed by several more scenes that keep her character in the story until about 40 minutes into the film. At that point Davis's Miranda disappears with special effects and reappears as her daughter, played by Barbara Carrera. The remaining 50 minutes roll by with little mention of her character until the final scenes, during an exorcism in which some dubbing and special effects are used to rid the world of the witches in the storyline. In total, she appears on-screen for a total of approximately 15 minutes.

In fact, in the original script, the entire opening of the final film featuring Tom Bosley does not appear. The feature begins with Camp and Rasche heading home from the airport for their first encounter with Bette's Miranda.

With the movie finished, the next challenge would be to get it released. Cohen had persuaded MGM to finance the picture. Now, he had to persuade them to release it. "By the time we had finished the picture, the company was up for sale," said Cohen. "The director of marketing was gone, none of the executives who had approved it were still with the company."

Cohen had experienced a similar situation at Warner Bros. with his film *It's Alive* in the 1970s and claimed that this time, no one at MGM wanted to spend any money on distributing, promoting, or marketing *Wicked Stepmother*.

Ironically, had Davis died before the completion the film likely would have garnered more attention as the star's final feature.

In the end, however, Cohen never was fully satisfied with the direction the studio chose, but Cohen did his best to promote his film. "I did many interviews prior to the release of the picture, after Bette went public about her reaction to the film (which she hadn't seen). Though she fabricated stories about how I'd mistreated her, I spoke of her only with admiration," said Cohen.

Even though the suggestion of a wide release was nixed, Cohen got his theatrical premiere with the feature opening in late January 1989. "They opened it in New Orleans during Mardi Gras week," said Cohen. "As you can imagine, it didn't do an awful lot of business."

Bette tried to distance herself and refused to see the final picture. "I would be ashamed to have people think I sanctioned something like this," Bette said of the film's release. Costar Lionel Stander backed her up. "Like Miss Davis herself said, the script could have been better."

"She was still fiery, she never stopped being Bette Davis," noted Stander. "But her face ... ravaged, up on the big screen ... you felt sorry for her."

While the lackluster premiere didn't garner the attention of Hollywood, or draw a plethora of stars to its opening night, it was not a total loss. The Mardi Gras premiere was highlighted by a Bette Davis lookalike contest in one theater and at another opening there was an offer of free admission to any patron who brought along Bette Davis memorabilia. The second promotion did stipulate that seating was limited and would be on a first-come, first-served basis.

Promotions and offers of free admittance, however, didn't help *Wicked Stepmother* in its limited release. Even the ranting of its irate star did not interest many moviegoers to show up at the theater. It sank quickly in release with a last-place finish in its opening week at the box office after premiering in more theaters on February 3, 1989. It earned a miserable $43,749 at its 195 theaters, averaging out to about $224 per screen. Films like *The Fly II, Sleepaway Camp III* and *Major League* fared better with moviegoers during the release.

With the film's poor showing there was little hope of MGM agreeing to expand the release nationally or internationally and possibly even less hope of any theater picking up the film even if MGM had offered it. On the other hand, a film Bette very much wanted to star in, *Driving Miss Daisy*, was released months later, earning Jessica Tandy an Oscar for the part Bette coveted. The film would win Best Picture at the Academy Awards in 1990, and Tandy would earn the distinction as the oldest winner in history to win the Oscar for Best Actress.

Bette moved on from the film, and in her frail health knew that her days of location shoots, action sequences, and long hours on Hollywood sound stages were running out. She simply didn't have the stamina. At best she might manage guest appearances or cameo roles if she were lucky enough to be offered the opportunity.

In January 1989, even before *Wicked Stepmother*'s release, Bette collapsed while appearing at the 6th Annual American Cinema Awards, later discovering that her cancer had returned. Even so, that year she managed personal appearances on two talk shows that April, *Late Night with David Letterman* and an interview on the *Today* show. Days later, she would be honored during the Film Society of Lincoln Center Annual Gala Tribute.

At the end of September that year, she felt strong enough to fly to the Spain to be awarded for her lifetime achievements during the Donostia-San Sebastian International Film Festival. In Basque for the festivities, she was boosted by the attention and admiration; but all the activity took a toll and her health again began to fail. Too ill to fly back to the United States, her lawyer Harold Schiff said, "The doctors told us the cancer had spread, that it was terminal. The doctors had said let her go on going about her business."

She flew to the French commune of Neuilly-sur-Seine, just west of Paris, accompanied by her assistant Kathryn Sermak. Sermak would be with Bette during the last days of her life. She said it was in the hospital that Bette was told by doctors that her breast cancer, which had been in remission for five years, had "exploded," and she didn't have long to live.

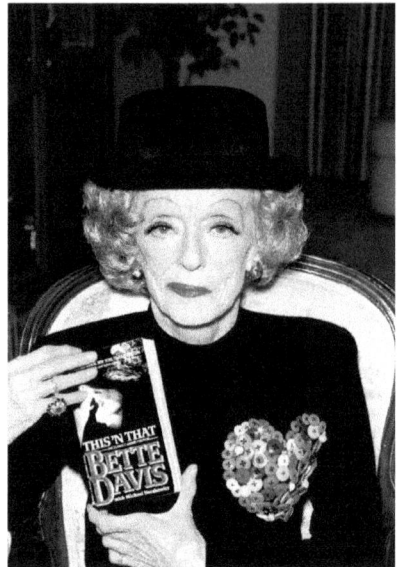

"Miss D accepted it," Sermak wrote in her book *Miss D and Me: Life with the Invincible Bette Davis.* "She told me to call [her son] Michael and then [her lawyer and friend] Harold. She did not ask me to reach out to B.D.[her daughter]. She had her moments with them over the phone, comforting those she loved so deeply. She did not want them to come because she did not want 'this bedraggled body and the look of death' to be their last memory of her. She was not worried that I would have the same trouble. 'They don't see me every day like you do, Kath,'" Sermak wrote.

On Oct. 6, 1989, at the American Hospital of Paris, Sermak held Davis's hand in her final moments. "I squeezed her hand, hoping she would squeeze back as she had those days in the hospital after the stroke, but I got no response," she wrote.

She passed away about 11:30 p.m. that day. She was 81 years old. She would later be interred at Forest Lawn Hollywood Hills Cemetery in Los Angeles beside her mother and sister, as she had long wished.

She left an estate estimated at nearly $1 million, which was split between her caretaker and assistant Kathryn Sermak, and her son, Michael Merrill. Her daughters and grandchildren were left out of the will.

While it sounded like a lot of money, it wasn't. "Let's face it, even though Bette had been one of the biggest stars in the history of motion pictures, at this late stage of her career she desperately needed a job. In fact, Bette didn't have a great deal of money when she died. She left around $1 million, which included her apartment and that was probably worth $750,000. So Bette only had something like $250,000 in the whole world," said Cohen.

Before Bette died that fall, she was hoping that a wider audience would never have the chance to view her final feature. The film's small theatrical release and dismal performance almost made it so. However, MGM already had planned a video release for the film and, ironically enough, with her death, they tied *Wicked Stepmother*'s video debut into the release of some of Davis's greatest screen classics with the "Bette Davis Signature Collection," which included winners like *Jezebel, The Letter* and *Now, Voyager*, among others. However, even positioned there, the movie didn't garner much attention, and the film was called "a mess" and Davis was singled out for her terrible appearance. One reviewer wrote, "The only perverse point of interest was Davis's wraithlike appearance, which the actress herself predicted would cause her fans to be 'horrified'."

Davis fans did find their way to accept the film, which was a relief to Cohen. "I never meant Bette Davis any harm. Just the opposite."

Though not high on anyone's list of memorable performances for a Hollywood legend, the film wasn't the failure many claimed it was, said the director. "Many perceived *Wicked Stepmother* to be a financial failure. Apparently not. I ran into the attorney for the insurance company several years back, who informed me that he'd just received a check for $780,000 in profits," reported Cohen years after the release. "The completion guarantor, Film Finances, got a similar amount. I'm sure they've been issued additional checks since, which means they've

recouped their entire investment and are happily in the black. Had I simply thrown in the towel and collected my salary, the studio, the insurance company, and the guarantor would have eaten the entire budget."

Bette Davis's name, reputation, and eyes succeeded even when the odds were against them. It was a wicked end to a wondrous career.

21

"I am doomed to an eternity of compulsive work. No set goal achieved satisfies. Success only breeds a new goal. The golden apple devoured has seeds. It is endless."

- Bette Davis

Chapter 21

The Original Script

*S**am is an aging widower who lives with his daughter Jenny and
her husband Steven. Returning from vacation, Jenny and Steve
discover Sam has gotten married on a whim and upon their
arrival the couple find their new "wicked" stepmother has moved in and
taken over their home, changed their father, and has set out on ruining
their lives. They eventually discover their new stepmother, Miranda, is
not an ordinary old woman - she's a witch and is using her evil powers to
divide and conquer everyone around them.*

...

The original script for *Wicked Stepmother* was an original story
and screenplay by Larry Cohen. Dated for the 1989 film shoot, the
original screenplay offers a clear picture of what the director/producer
had in mind when he crafted his Bette Davis movie. Accepted by Bette
Davis, the original script largely centers on the character of Miranda, the
witch played by Davis as she sets her sites on taking over the lives,
home, and money of the Miller family. While it appears that Cohen did
make allowances for Bette's health by limiting her actions and allowing
many of the other actors to move around her, the star was featured in the
bulk of the film.

Once Davis abandoned the movie, Cohen held onto the footage he'd shot of the star, but took to the script with a delicate hand, hoping to retain much of the original intent and humor as he shifted the remaining two-thirds of the story away from Miranda and onto the other actors. For Jenny and Steve Miller (renamed Fisher in the completed film), played by Colleen Camp and David Rasche, their characters and dialogue were only adjusted slightly to accommodate their interactions with Priscilla rather than Miranda, and the trajectory of their characters remained the same. The biggest shift came from the focus on Miranda' moving to that of her daughter Priscilla, played by Barbara Carrera. Carrera would take on the bulk of the work, having Cohen move the role of the primary witch to Priscilla. With Carrera playing the young and beautiful daughter of Miranda, scenes involving her acting with Camp and Rasche, as well as Steve and Jenny's son Mike were altered. In fact, Mike's character, played by Shawn Donohue, is somewhat reduced. Cohen's original story had several key scenes for Mike to interact with his new grandmother and to explore the relationship between Miranda and her new grandson. Several of the scenes shift to Priscilla, but much of the energy was lost and Priscilla spends most of her time engaging with Steve in a quest for his love.

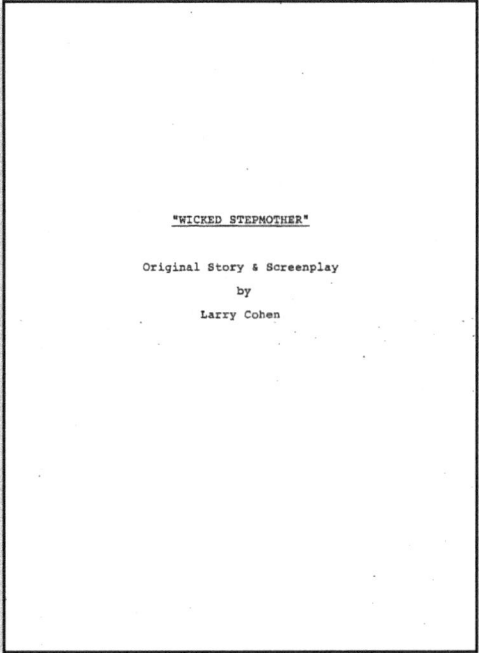

"WICKED STEPMOTHER"

Original Story & Screenplay
by
Larry Cohen

In the finished film the Miller family is changed to the Fisher family and all the scenes between Miranda and Priscilla are dropped and replaced by extending existing scenes or creating a new avenue for Priscilla to advance her space in the story. The idea of Miranda taking over the family is relegated to the backstory, while Priscilla's intentions on splitting up Steve and Jenny are put front and center. In the original script a battle takes place between Miranda and Priscilla as Miranda begins to undermine Priscilla's attempts to win Steve over. Priscilla sees her mother's efforts as unacceptable and she begins to sabotage Miranda's plans.

For the original story, Cohen intended to start the film with Jenny and Steve, rather than a lengthy scene with Tom Bosley and Susie Garrett discovering Miranda's prior victims, who have been shrunk and dropped into a shoe box. After the opening and credits a police line-up of "old ladies" is held where the eyewitnesses cannot identify Davis' Miranda. Neither scene exists in the original script and the film opens this way:

> FADE IN: International Airline Terminal – Day
> The flight from Hawaii has just landed and returning tourists are staggering off the aircraft under the burden of momentous quantities of carry-on luggage, including cases of pineapples, sacks of coconuts, surf boards and scuba gear.
> Among them we focus on Steve Miller, a handsome fellow in his early thirties and his very pretty wife, Jenny.

While much of the dialogue is retained in the finished film, the new opening begins in a taxi with no scenes at the airport. The three scenes delay the arrival of Bette's Miranda until after the daughter and son-in-law arrive home. The arrival, aside from some special effects to introduce Miranda as a villain not unlike Jason from *Friday the 13th* or Freddy in *Nightmare on Elm Street*, Bette arrives on queue to greet her new stepchildren.

The next sequence of film is largely intact with the script, with Bette engaging with the family and ruffling the feathers of Jenny. However, Bette failed to film a courtroom scene where she upturns all the paperwork during a court case, so we're introduced to Barbara Carrera who arrives unannounced to shake things up. Had Bette filmed the scene it would have been largely the same.

It's not until a third into the story when Miranda's daughter Priscilla officially arrives that the script takes a turn. In the original screenplay, Miranda welcomes the arrival of her daughter and plans a large family meal for everyone to get to know one another. Without Bette, Cohen uses special effects to simultaneously illustrate the removal of Miranda and the arrival of Priscilla on the doorstep.

In the original screenplay, Priscilla's arrival is not dramatically changed but Miranda is removed from the scene. The script goes this way:

> The doorbell rings again. Steve crosses to the window and yells out.
>
> Steve: Who's down there?
>
> Voice: Priscilla. Is my mother there?
>
> Steve: Priscilla who?
>
> Miranda: My Priscilla! Come to visit.
>
> Jenny: Oh, no.
>
> Miranda: I wrote to her, but I never thought she'd appear. You're going to love her.
>
> Cut to interior foyer – downstairs – night

The front door is opened to reveal Priscilla. Jenny and Miranda are still coming downstairs. Steve has opened the door and he's completely knocked out at the sight he beholds.

Bette Davis is largely kept in the story for the first 40 minutes of the film, though she only appears in less than half of the first third. When she vanishes with some special effects that dissolve her character, Priscilla arrives on the doorstep, and we are now able to connect that Miranda and Priscilla are working together, and the earlier courtroom scene was actually Miranda's plan.

In Priscilla's entrance some of the dialogue was reworked to remove the need for Bette, and Miranda's mischievous cat, Pericles, appears at the top of the stairs to be picked up by Priscilla, who refers to her as "Mommy." In the original story, Miranda's plan would have had her transforming Pericles into her beautiful daughter. In the rework, Priscilla enters Miranda's bedroom and we never see Bette again. Pericles appears several other times as a substitution for Bette to keep some elements of the story going.

In the original script Miranda and Priscilla meet for the first time in the entryway.

> Wider Shot. Foyer – Night.
> Miranda embraces her daughter.
> Priscilla: Why, you haven't changed at all, Mother.
> Miranda: You certainly have. All of a sudden you're a big girl.
> Steve: She sure is.
> Priscilla: I can only stay a few weeks.
> Jenny: There goes the bedroom.

Miranda: Nonsense. Priscilla will bunk with me. We have so much to catch up on. Let me introduce everyone. Meet Steve and Jenny, my new kids.

Other scenes, like the one in which Camp tosses a bucket of water onto Carrera, hoping Priscilla will melt like the witch in *The Wizard of Oz*, were originally intended for Bette, but the reactions and

---

45. Cont.   17 ·

                         JENNY
              He's accustomed to his own room. He
              has some rights, too.

                         SAM
              So blame me!

                         STEVE
              Why don't we wait till Mike gets
              back from my folks and let him make
              the decision.

                         JENNY
              What decision. I think Miranda has
              made all the decisions for us.

                         SAM
              Could we talk later? I think one of
              my programs is coming on.

              And he hurries downstairs again. Jenny turns to her
              husband.

                         JENNY
              I want to talk to you.

              She walks into the bedroom. He follows her. He slams the
              door shut.

46. INT. THE BEDROOM

              They're alone now.

                         JENNY
              The nerve.

                         STEVE
              Listen, your mother wasn't any
              picnic as I recall. You never got
              along with her either.

                         JENNY
              Are you comparing that creature to
              my mother?

                         STEVE
              Well, you fought like cats and dogs.
              You didn't even speak for a year.

                         JENNY
              I won't listen to this.

                                                          Cont.

dialogue are largely the same. Some scenes, like a scene where Miranda manages to get most of the family to pick up her smoking habit, and a scene with children arriving at the doorstep on Halloween to be greeted by Bette Davis' Miranda were dropped.

20. CLOSEUP - JENNY

                              JENNY
                    Oh, my God.

     CAMERA PANS TO Steve, his reaction, then:

                              STEVE
                    Do I smell something burning?

21. WIDER ANGLE

     Sam still looking sheepishly away from them. Behind him in
     the doorway to the kitchen a puff of smoke appears. CAMERA
     BEGINS TO DOLLY FORWARD toward that kitchen door as a figure
     steps into view, puffing away vigorously on a cigarette.
     There's a halo of smoke about her as MIRANDA comes into full
     view.

     She eyes the new arrivals for just an instant before
     speaking.

                              MIRANDA
                    Call me Mom.

22. TWO SHOT - JENNY AND STEVE

     Jenny looking on in abject horror. Jenny is speechless.

                              STEVE
                            (whispers)
                    Honey, she's smoking.

                              JENNY
                    In our house.

23. MED. SHOT - SAM

     looking helplessly back at Miranda. A puff of smoke ENTERS
     THE FRAME, enveloping him, as Miranda steps in beside him,
     putting her arm around his shoulder. Sam just stands there
     like a lump, letting it happen. Miranda inhales deeply,
     flicks an ash carelessly on the carpet.

                              MIRANDA
                    I can't tell you how wonderful it
                    is to be part of a family again.

24. CLOSEUP - JENNY

                              JENNY
                    She's flicking ashes.

The conclusion of the film is altered as well, with Miranda's marriage to Sam being deemed invalid because she's still married to Priscilla's father – a demon. In the re-worked version, Jenny uses spells to drive Priscilla into the cat already inhabited by Miranda and destroys her house in the process. The story was similar to the original except much of the drama pits Miranda against Priscilla as they split the house apart. A demon arrives and transforms Priscilla back into the cat and Miranda realizes the gig is up and picks up her cat and leaves the home, only to try to pick up the cab driver as she is driving away. However, before she leaves, Cohen intended one more tribute remark from Bette.

> "She regards the place from top to bottom – with disdain. Then doing her best imitation of Bette Davis, she mutters:
> Miranda: "What a dump."

The 115-page script concludes the film with a freeze frame of a "flirtatious Miranda," as the film ends. In the re-worked version Cohen offers a roll call of the players in the film, ending with Bette Davis saying, "Call me Mama" and blowing smoke across the camera. The following pages offers snippets of the script, highlighting key scenes where the scene shifted away from Davis once she exited the films. The original script offers and idea of how the original film might have played out had Davis not left the role.

> PROSECUTOR
> We'd like to move for a postponement.

> JUDGE
> Denied! Case dismissed. Next
> case, please.

The defendants jump up and shake Steve's hand. The
Prosecutor is fuming.

> PROSECUTOR
> (to Steve)
> I don't know how <u>you</u> did this.

> STEVE
> I didn't do anything.

Steve starts up the aisle. Miranda is standing there
waiting for him.

> MIRANDA
> Congratulations are in order.

> STEVE
> When you walked in that door and
> Jessup's papers blow all over the
> place. It was classic.

> MIRANDA
> I suppose I was disruptive.

> STEVE
> It wasn't your fault

> MIRANDA
> Oh, but it was. <u>All my fault.</u>

> STEVE
> It was?

> MIRANDA
> Aren't you going to buy me lunch?
> It appears that you have nothing
> left to do today.

> STEVE
> That's not a bad idea.

> MIRANDA
> How about splitting a nice blood
> rare steak?

> STEVE
> If you promise not to tell Jenny.

                                                          Cont.

FADE IN:

1. INT. AIRLINE TERMINAL - DAY

    The flight from Hawaii has just landed and returning
    tourists are staggering off the aircraft under the burden of
    momentous quantities of carry-on luggage, including cases of
    pineapples, sacks of coconuts, surfboards and scuba gear.

    Among them we focus on STEVE MILLER, a handsome fellow in
    his early thirties and his very pretty wife, JENNY.

                         STEVE
               We could've taken a later flight
               and had the whole day on the beach.

                         JENNY
               I don't know. I'm worried about
               Dad.

                         STEVE
               He sounded fine on the phone.

                         JENNY
               It's the first time he's been left
               alone since Mom died.

2. EXT. THE AIRPORT - DAY

    Steve and Jenny piling their luggage into the trunk of a
    TAXICAB. The DRIVER does little to assist them with the
    bags but eavesdrops intently on their conversation.

                         STEVE
               If my parents can take care of
               Mikey for two whole weeks--why
               can't your father stay home and
               look after one little dog?

                         TAXI DRIVER
                         (butting in)
               That don't sound like a lot to ask.

    Steve and Jenny pause to glare at the driver who reluctantly
    takes his place behind the wheel.

                         JENNY
               I didn't say he couldn't. I just
               have a bad feeling.

231. Cont.

                         MIRANDA
          I didn't plan for you to leave so
          soon.

                         JENNY
          Yes, well it seems I'm the only one
          around her that you don't control.

                         MIRANDA
          I never wanted you.

                         JENNY
          Get out of my way.

                         MIRANDA
          Not even going to wait to kiss Steve
          and Mikey goodbye? They'll be back
          from the game soon.

                         JENNY
          Sorry, Miranda, no big scenes for
          you to gloat over. I'm calling a
          taxi and then I'm gone.

                         MIRANDA
          Quitter!

     Miranda exits into another part of the house as Jenny dials
     for her cab.

232. INT. DINING ROOM - DAY

     Priscilla is at the table Clipping pictures ouf of "House
     Beautiful." She's wearing Jenny's sexiest dress which she's
     permanently appropriated. Now Miranda enters radiating
     fury.

                         MIRANDA
          Who told you you could move into the
          master suite with Steve?

                         PRISCILLA
          I don't have to be told. I'm a
          grown woman now, Mother.

                         MIRANDA
          Not when you're operating under one
          of my spells, you're not.

                         PRISCILLA
          Now, don't try to manipulate me like
          the others.

                                             Cont.

271. ANGLE ON JEROME

running into the house, darting between their legs, he
rushes hungrily to the big pot and before he can be stopped,
he proceeds to lap up the contents of the cauldron.

                    STEVE
            Don't. That's Max!

                    JENNY
            He ate "Max."

The dog looks up at his family, happily licks his
chops--then barks. But it isn't a bark, its A ROAR--like
something coming out of the alien in a sci-fi epic. The
Miller family stand frozen, staring at their pet--not quite
sure that their troubles are over.

                    STEVE
                    (timidly)
            Okay, Jerome. Good dog. From
            now on you can stay inside again,
            okay?

The dog roars again. The house trembles.

                                        CUT TO:

272. EXT. PARKWAY - NIGHT

The taxi carrying Miranda and her Cat "Pericles" speeds by.

273. INT. TAXI - NIGHT

Miranda leans forward, studies the elderly driver's name on
his hack license. Then puts on all her charm.

                    MIRANDA
            Well, Maurice...do you own your
            own cab?

She's still just looking for a home. She pops a cigarette
between in her teeth. It lights by itself. Pericles curls
up happily on her lap--and hisses her approval.

FREEZE FRAME on a flirtatious Miranda--and

                                        FADE OUT.

                    THE END

---

45. Cont.

                    JENNY
            He's accustomed to his own room. He
            has some rights, too.

                    SAM
            So blame me!

                    STEVE
            Why don't we wait till Mike gets
            back from my folks and let him make
            the decision.

                    JENNY
            What decision. I think Miranda has
            made all the decisions for us.

                    SAM
            Could we talk later? I think one of
            my programs is coming on.

And he hurries downstairs again. Jenny turns to her
husband.

                    JENNY
            I want to talk to you.

She walks into the bedroom. He follows her. He slams the
door shut.

46. INT. THE BEDROOM

They're alone now.

                    JENNY
            The nerve.

                    STEVE
            Listen, your mother wasn't any
            picnic as I recall. You never got
            along with her either.

                    JENNY
            Are you comparing that creature to
            my mother?

                    STEVE
            Well, you fought like cats and dogs.
            You didn't even speak for a year.

                    JENNY
            I won't listen to this.

                                        Cont.

285

267. Cont.

The gross demon seems to float around the living room. It's long snake-like body and head coiling back now, intimidating poor Priscilla, who begins to shrink down in submission.

                    PRISCILLA (cont'd)
          Meow. Meow.

She begins making catlike noises. Then she curls up on the floor. That long nubile tail pops out from under her dress. The whiskers again sprout forth on her cheeks. This time Priscilla realizes it's happening to her.

Jerome, the dog, peeks in from outside through a crack in the wall and curiously watches Priscilla transformed.

                    MIRANDA
          That's better. Getting back into
          character.

                    PRISCILLA
                    (transforming)
          Mommy, don't make me. Daddy, I
          didn't mean to be bad.

The demon's VOICE is heard now and the room trembles.

                    DEMON
          Do as your mother tells you. I
          don't like to be bothered.

                    JENNY
                    (points to demon)
          That's Daddy!

CAMERA PANS to include Sam who's just entered the room, all spruced up with his hair slicked back with Vasoline. He has seen what's going on. He's outraged!

                    SAM
          I want a divorce.

                    MIRANDA
          Now, wait a minute, Samuel.

                    SAM
          Wait a minute, nothing. You're
          married to this guy, you can't be
          married to me.

                    MIRANDA
          Well, daddy's not exactly a person. I
          only invoke him when it's absolutely
          necessary. He's not much of a
          companion.

                                        Cont.

22

"I charmed her into signing on, got her a paycheck, and gave her cast approval. Everything to make her happy. And what happened made her miserable."

- Larry Cohen, Writer/Director of *Wicked Stepmother*

Chapter 22

Closing Remarks

For the last 25 years of Bette Davis's life and career, after the filming of **What Ever Happened to Baby Jane?**, a disproportionate number of her films, and numerous television projects - fell into a horror genre. Unfortunately for her, the films worsened as they progressed. From **Baby Jane** to **Hush ... Hush, Sweet Charlotte; Dead Ringer; Nanny;** to some extent **The Anniversary; Burnt Offerings; Return From Witch Mountain** and **Watcher in the Woods,** among them - each is arguably each worse than the prior film.

For a legend of the silver screen, these markers or milestones are not what one hopes for as a cap to a nearly 60-year career in the movies. While some might suggest that **Wicked Stepmother** is a black comedy and fails to qualify as a horror film, historians might suggest that it was this series of latter horror films that inspired **Wicked Stepmother** in the *first place, and the film represents a spoof or iconic look at the last third of Davis's career. In many ways, the reason the film itself could be deemed a failure is in large part because the films and Davis's allure as a grand dame of Grand Guignol genre had lost its steam.*

...

During a scene in *Mr. Skeffington*, Claude Rains tells his wife that a woman is beautiful when she's loved. Davis retorts, as only Bette Davis can, "A woman is beautiful when she has eight hours' sleep and goes to the beauty parlor every day. And bone structure has a lot to do with it, too."

The words held as much truth for her character as they did for her. While beauty, as she saw it, is not that hard to obtain, especially if it comes in your DNA, it is not a sign of character. In some ways, it was how Davis saw her career opposite Joan Crawford. Davis called Crawford a star, while she saw herself as an actress. As a pretty chorus girl, Crawford could carve a career out on her looks, but Davis felt it was her talent that would sustain her. Without the glamour-girl face or figure, she knew her capabilities as an actress, combined with drive and determination, would make her a force to be reckoned with. She was right.

Though Bette Davis is no longer with us and hasn't been for more than 30 years, her legend lives on. The feuds with actresses like Joan Crawford or friendships with Olivia de Havilland, and the battles with Warner Bros. - Jack Warner in particular - are legendary. Her on-screen moments and off-screen dramas captured our imaginations for decades.

Even her death became a performance to remember. Though dying of cancer and taking everything she had to just walk, Bette gathered every ounce of strength to fly 6,000 miles from Los Angeles to a San Sebastian, Spain to a film festival in order to accept an award for her lifetime of work.

Bette Davis longed to bask in the limelight once more and feel the adulation of her fans and fellow actors. Reporters and photographers pushed to get close to her, and the film community paid tribute to the work she dedicated her life to, but within a few short days she was worn out and her body was failing her. Cancer was overwhelming her body.

Flown to Paris, Bette Davis died three days later.

Though she is gone, she is certainly not forgotten. Now, decades after her death, we are still talking about her.

More books have been written about Davis than nearly every other actress - perhaps with the exception of Marilyn Monroe. Those who knew her and worked with her offered their own observations. Documentaries and series television have looked at the legend with varying levels of success.

As a relatively public persona, Bette Davis's life is well known and chronicled, but who she really was, in some ways, remains a mystery. She was a cultivated personality born from a time when Hollywood created its stars and crafted their lives. While much of Bette's Hollywood persona was indeed defined by her, the publicity machine behind her helped shape and mold the star she would ultimately become. As she aged, she formed a hardened shell around the persona of Bette Davis and inhabited elements of the characters she played. The outspoken, rebellious actress of the 1940s and 50s would become as much a part of her as the cigarette that hung from the corner of her mouth. The batting eyes, the pursed lips and the dynamic speech patterns became embedded within her. In some ways, they even became exaggerated in her later years, becoming something of a caricature of herself.

Some of her films live on, more due to her name and face than for their contributions to the evolution of the cinema. While some of her films like *Jezebel*; *The Little Foxes*; and *Now, Voyager* stand testament to cinema at its best, other films like *Dead Ringer, The Anniversary,* or *The Nanny* remain cult classics due to her star turn in them. *Wicked Stepmother* can be counted among the latter.

While Bette Davis - and likely many of her most ardent fans - would have wished *Wicked Stepmother* hadn't become her final cinematic feature, it is ironic that it is. Had she ended her career on *The Whales of August,* she might have left her career on one of her finest and most subtle performances in a film that was better for having her captured by its cameras. However, Davis would have none of it.

"I remember that later Bette was quoted in the *New York Times* as saying, 'I have dealt with many directors in my career, but in Larry Cohen I have met my Waterloo!'" Larry Cohen remembered. "I thought that was cute. I found out that Bette was appearing at The New York Film Festival at Lincoln Center, so I sent a bouquet of flowers to her hotel with a card saying: "From your Waterloo."

Her final film would reach its widest audience in 1989 when *Wicked Stepmother* was released in time for Halloween on home video.

Cohen was happy to have the film at last find an audience. Even with all the drama, he was proud of the work. "I'm glad I made the film, despite all the chaos and subterfuge that went on. If I had to do it all again I would, because I enjoyed having Bette as an acquaintance and having her at least appear to like me. I certainly liked her. I guess that, ultimately, it was my fault, because I was the one who hired her. I was the one who insisted on going ahead and making *Wicked Stepmother* with Bette despite certain people advising me against it. I've thought a lot about this over the years and I now realize that on one level, I simply couldn't accept the fact that Bette Davis could no longer be in movies. I was such a big fan of hers, maybe I just wanted to prove all those people wrong. I wanted to bring some of that old magic back to the movies."

For Cohen, it was merely a bump in the road of a long career. His 1974 film, *It's Alive*, was probably his most memorable and iconic motion picture. About a murdering mutant baby, it resembled a cult version of *Rosemary's Baby*, and Cohen landed legendary composer Bernard Herrmann to provide the musical score. Herrmann was best known for his moving work with Alfred Hitchcock on countless suspense classics. In fact, Herrman was scheduled to score Cohen's next picture, *God Told Me To*, but after a screening of the picture and dinner with Cohen, Herrmann returned to his hotel and died of an apparent heart attack in his sleep. Cohen would dedicate his film to the composer.

After Herrmann, Bette would be perhaps the biggest star to work on one of his films. After *Wicked Stepmother* he would go on to greater success, mostly as a writer, with films like the thriller *Phone Booth*, in 2002 which starred Colin Farrell's, and the 2004 film *Cellular*, starring Chris Evans and Kim Basinger.

Reflecting on his career, years later, he said "It wasn't just going to the studio like a factory laborer and making pictures and going home every night. We were out there in the jungle making these movies, improvising, and having fun, and creating movies from out of thin air without much money. When he died in March, 2019 at the age of 77, there was little mention of his work on *Wicked Stepmother*, but for him, the chance to work with Bette Davis, was a career highlight.

As for Bette, retiring was a word she failed to recognize and even as others in the business saw her ability to work was becoming a challenge, she refused to accept it. "I lah-h-h-v my profession," she told one interviewer not long before her death. "I would n-e-e-e-ver stop. Relax? I relax when I work. It's my life."

Even if her stamina had been strong the roles for which she was suited were becoming few and far between.

So, she left us with *Wicked Stepmother,* a film created solely with her in mind. While the film itself may not be up to the standards Davis set for herself, the story behind the film illustrates the determination and strength of a woman who dedicated her life to the art of the film. For that we can be grateful.

23

"If everyone likes you, you're not doing it right."

- Bette Davis

Chapter 23

Bette Davis Filmography

1980s

- *1989 Wicked Stepmother - Miranda Pierpoint*
- *1987 The Whales of August - Libby Strong*
- *1986 As Summers Die (TV Movie) - Hannah Loftin*
- *1985 Murder with Mirrors (TV Movie) - Carrie Louise Serrocold*
- *1983 Right of Way (TV Movie) - Mini Dwyer*
- *1983 Hotel (TV Series) - Laura Trent*
- *1982 Little Gloria... Happy at Last (TV Movie) - Alice Gwynne Vanderbilt*
- *1982 A Piano for Mrs. Cimino (TV Movie) - Esther McDonald Cimino*
- *1981 Family Reunion (TV Movie) - Elizabeth Winfield*
- *1980 Skyward (TV Movie) - Billie Dupree*
- *1980 The Watcher in the Woods - Mrs. Aylwood*
- *1980 White Mama (TV Movie) - Adele Malone*

1970s

- 1979 Strangers: The Story of a Mother and Daughter (TV Movie) - Lucy Mason
- 1978 Death on the Nile - Mrs. Van Schuyler
- 1978 Return from Witch Mountain - Letha
- 1978 The Dark Secret of Harvest Home (TV Mini-Series) - Widow Fortune
- 1977 Laugh-In (TV Series) - Guest star
- 1976 The Disappearance of Aimee (TV Movie) - Minnie Kennedy
- 1976 Burnt Offerings - Aunt Elizabeth
- 1974 Hello Mother, Goodbye! (TV Movie)
- 1973 Scream, Pretty Peggy (TV Movie) - Mrs. Elliott
- 1972 The Judge and Jake Wyler (TV Movie) - Judge Meredith
- 1972 The Scopone Game - The Millionairess
- 1972 Madame Sin - Madame Sin
- 1971 Bunny O'Hare - Bunny O'Hare
- 1970 Connecting Rooms - Wanda Fleming
- 1970 It Takes a Thief (TV Series) - Bessie Grindel

1960s

- 1968 The Anniversary - Mrs. Taggart
- 1966 Gunsmoke (TV Series) - Etta Stone
- 1965 The Nanny - Nanny
- 1965 The Decorator (TV Short) - Liz

- *1964 Hush...Hush, Sweet Charlotte - Charlotte Hollis*
- *1964 Where Love Has Gone - Mrs. Gerald Hayden*
- *1964 Dead Ringer - Margaret DeLorca / Edith Phillips*
- *1963 The Empty Canvas - Dino's mother*
- *1963 Perry Mason (TV Series) - Constant Doyle*
- *1962 The Virginian (TV Series) - Celia Miller*
- *1962 What Ever Happened to Baby Jane? - Baby Jane Hudson*
- *1959-1961 Wagon Train (TV Series)*
- *   - The Bettina May Story (1961) - Bettina May*
- *   - The Elizabeth McQueeny Story (1959) - Elizabeth McQueeny*
- *   - The Ella Lindstrom Story (1959) - Ella Lindstrom*
- *1961 Pocketful of Miracles - Apple Annie*

1950s

- *1959 The DuPont Show with June Allyson (TV Series) - Sarah Whitney*
- *1959 The Scapegoat - Countess*
- *1959 John Paul Jones - Empress Catherine the Great*
- *1959 Alfred Hitchcock Presents (TV Series) - Miss Fox*
- *1958 Suspicion (TV Series) - Mrs. Wilfred Ellis*
- *1957-1958 General Electric Theater (TV Series)*
  - *The Cold Touch (1958) ... Christine Marlowe*
  - *With Malice Toward One (1957) ... Miss Burrows*

- *1958 Studio 57 (TV Series)*
- *1957 Telephone Time (TV Series) - Mrs. Beatrice Enter*
- *1957 The Ford Television Theatre (TV Series) - Dolley Madison*
- *1957 Schlitz Playhouse (TV Series) - Irene Wagner*
- *1956 Storm Center - Alicia Hull*
- *1956 The Catered Affair - Mrs. Agnes Hurley*
- *1956 The 20th Century-Fox Hour (TV Series) - Marie Hoke*
- *1955 The Virgin Queen - Queen Elizabeth I*
- *1952 The Star - Margaret Elliot*
- *1952 All Star Revue (TV Series) - Guest Actress*
- *1952 Phone Call from a Stranger - Marie Hoke*
- *1951 Another Man's Poison - Janet Frobisher*
- *1951 Payment on Demand - Joyce Ramsey (nee Jackson)*
- *1950 All About Eve - Margo Channing*

1940s

- *1949 Beyond the Forest - Rosa Moline*
- *1948 June Bride - Linda Gilman*
- *1948 Winter Meeting - Susan Grieve*
- *1946 Deception - Christine Radcliffe*
- *1946 A Stolen Life - Kate Bosworth / Patricia Bosworth*
- *1945 The Corn Is Green - Miss Lilly Moffat*
- *1944 Hollywood Canteen - Bette Davis*
- *1944 Mr. Skeffington - Fanny Trellis Skeffington*

- *1943 Old Acquaintance - Kit Marlowe*
- *1943 Thank Your Lucky Stars - Bette Davis*
- *1943 Watch on the Rhine - Sara Muller*
- *1942 Now, Voyager - Charlotte Vale*
- *1942 In This Our Life - Stanley Timberlake*
- *1942 The Man Who Came to Dinner - Maggie Cutler*
- *1941 The Little Foxes - Regina Giddens*
- *1941 The Bride Came C.O.D. - Joan Winfield*
- *1941 Shining Victory - Nurse (uncredited)*
- *1941 The Great Lie - Maggie Patterson*
- *1940 The Letter - Leslie Crosbie*
- *1940 All This, and Heaven Too - Henriette Deluzy-Desportes*
- *1940 If I Forget You (Short) - Bette Davis*

1930s

- *1939 The Private Lives of Elizabeth and Essex - Queen Elizabeth*
- *1939 The Old Maid - Charlotte Lovell*
- *1939 Juarez - Carlota of Mexico*
- *1939 Dark Victory - Judith Traherne*
- *1938 The Sisters - Louise Elliott*
- *1938 Jezebel - Julie Marsden*
- *1937 It's Love I'm After - Joyce Arden*
- *1937 That Certain Woman - Mary Donnell*

- *1937 Kid Galahad - Louise 'Fluff' Phillips*
- *1937 A Day at Santa Anita (Short) - (uncredited)*
- *1937 Marked Woman - Mary Dwight Strauber*
- *1936 Satan Met a Lady - Valerie Purvis*
- *1936 The Golden Arrow - Daisy Appleby*
- *1936 The Petrified Forest - Gabrielle Maple*
- *1935 Dangerous - Joyce Heath*
- *1935 Special Agent - Julie Gardner*
- *1935 Front Page Woman - Ellen Garfield*
- *1935 The Girl from 10th Avenue - Miriam A. Brady*
- *1935 Bordertown - Marie Roark*
- *1934 Housewife - Patricia Berkeley*
- *1934 Of Human Bondage - Mildred Rogers*
- *1934 Fog Over Frisco - Arlene Bradford*
- *1934 Jimmy the Gent - Joan Martin*
- *1934 Fashions of 1934 - Lynn Mason*
- *1934 The Big Shakedown - Norma Nelson*
- *1933 Bureau of Missing Persons - Norma Roberts*
- *1933 Ex-Lady - Helen Bauer*
- *1933 The Working Man - Jenny Hartland / Jane Grey*
- *1933 Parachute Jumper - Patricia 'Alabama' Brent*
- *1933 Just Around the Corner (Short) - Ginger*
- *1932 20,000 Years in Sing Sing - Fay Wilson*
- *1932 Three on a Match - Ruth Wescott*
- *1932 The Cabin in the Cotton - Madge Norwood*

- *1932 The Dark Horse - Kay Russell*
- *1932 The Rich Are Always with Us - Malbro*
- *1932 So Big! - Miss Dallas O'Mara*
- *1932 The Man Who Played God - Grace Blair*
- *1932 Hell's House - Peggy Gardner*
- *1932 The Menace - Peggy Lowell*
- *1931 Way Back Home - Mary Lucy*
- *1931 Waterloo Bridge - Janet Cronin*
- *1931 Seed - Margaret Carter*
- *1931 The Bad Sister - Laura Madison*

Sources

"I went back to work because someone had to pay for the groceries."

- Bette Davis

Bibliography

Selected Sources

A number of books, magazines, newspapers, documentaries and interviews provided sources of information and factual data that went into the writing of this book. Thank you to the many sources referenced throughout the book. There were many individuals whose work, insights, reviews, comments and suggestions that also helped make this book possible. The following are a collection of sources from books, magazines, newspapers and Internet sources that provided particular information and are recognized in the pages that follow.

Books

Andersen, Christopher P. *A Star, is a Star, Is a Star!* 1980. Doubleday and Company.

Brett, David. *Joan Crawford: Hollywood Martyr*. 2006. Da Capo Press.

Chandler, Charlotte. *Not the Girl Next Door*. 2008. Simon and Schuster.

Considine, Shaun. *Bette & Joan: The Divine Feud*. 1989. Dell Publishing.

Davis, Bette. *The Lonely Life*. 1962. G.P. Putnam's Sons.

Davis, Bette. *This 'n That*. 1987. Putnam Publishing Group.

Doyle, Michael. *Larry Cohen: The Stuff of Gods and Monsters*. 2016. BearManor Media.

Eames, John Douglas. *The MGM Story*. 1989. Portland House.

Finler, Joel. *The Hollywood Story*. 1988. Crown Publishers.

Guiles, Fred Lawrence. *Joan Crawford: The Last Word*. 1995. Birch Lane Press.

Hadleigh, Boze. *Scandals, Secrets and Swan Songs*. 2021. Lyon Press.

Higham, Charles. *The Life of Bette Davis*. 1981. MacMillan Publishing.

Hirschhorn, Clive. *The Universal Story*. 1983. Crown Publishers.

Israel, Lee. *Miss Tallulah Bankhead*. 1972. Berkley Books.

Johnes, Carl. *Crawford: The Last Years*. 1979. Dell Publishing.

McCarty, John. *Psychos: Eighty Years of Mad Movies, Maniacs, and Murderous Deeds*. 1986. St Martin's Press.

McCarty, John. The Fearmakers. 1994. St. Martin's Press.

Munn, Michael. *Jimmy Stewart - The Truth Behind the Legend*. 2006. Skyhorse Publishing.

Newquist, Roy. *Conversations With Joan Crawford*. 1980. Citadel Press.

Quirk, Lawrence J. and Schoell. *Joan Crawford: The Essential Biography*. 2002. The University Press of Kentucky.

Quirk, Lawrence J. *The Films of Joan Crawford*. 1971. Citadel Press.

Schoell, William. *Stay Out of the Shower*. 1985. Dembner Books.

Shelley, Peter. *Grand Dame Guignol Cinema*. 2009. McFarland & Company.

Shingler, Martin. *Women, Celebrity and Cultures of Ageing*. 2015. Palgrave Macmillan. London.

Skal, David. *The Monster Show*. 1993. Penguin Books.

Spada, James. *More Than a Woman*. 1993. Bantam Books.

Spada, James. *Peter Lawford: The Man Who Kept the Secrets*. 1991. Bantam Books.

Stallings, Penny. *Flesh and Fantasy*. 1978. St. Martin's Press.

Stine, Whitney. *I'd Love to Kiss You … Conversations with Bette Davis*. 1990. Pocket Books.

Thomas, Bob. *Joan Crawford*. 1978. Bantam Books.

Wayne, Jane Ellen. *Crawford's Men*. 1988. Prentice Hall Press.

Wilkerson, Tichi and Borie, Marcia. *Hollywood Legends*. 1988. Tale Weaver Publishing.

Articles, Magazines, Newspapers and Transcripts

Baker, Phil. "Joan Crawford: The Last Word Book Review." *Sunday Times*. April 7, 1996.

Barson, Michael. "From Hackwork to Highbrow Horror." *New York Times*. August 13, 1995.

Buchalter, Gail. "Kim Carnes' Inspiration Toasts 'their' Hit Record and Smiles with Bette Davis Eyes." *People*. July 6, 1981.

Cagle, Jess. "Joan Crawford: The Mildred Pierce Actress Saved Her Best Performance for Oscar Night." *Entertainment Weekly*. March, 1996.

Chambers, Andrea. "All About Bette." *People*. May 6, 1985.

Cohen, Larry. "I killed Bette Davis." *Film Comment*. July/August 2012

Coyle, Jake. "Larry Cohen, director of cult horror films, dies at 77." *Associated Press*. March 24, 2019.

Darrach, Brad. "Grand Dame, Grande Dame." *People*. October 23, 1989.

Eddy, Steve. "B-Movie Director Castle Looks Back in 'Step Right Up'." *The Orange County Register*. April 12, 1992.

Frye, William. "The Devil in Miss Davis." *Vanity Fair*. April 16, 2010.

Jackson, Kevin. "They Came from Beyond The Pale: Matinees Shamelessly Vulgar Hero is a Grade Z Horror Movie Producer of the 60s. But Which One?" *The Independent*. June 11, 1993.

Leonard, Tom. "My mother, Bette Davis, a DRUNKEN MONSTER who cast a demonic curse on her own family: The screen legend's daughter reignites the most toxic mother-daughter feud in Hollywood." *Daily Mail*. October 19, 2017.

Maslin, Janet. "There's a Horror Movie in Here!" *New York Times*. January 29, 1993.

Nehme, Farran Smith. "The Face of Bette Davis." *Film Comment*. March 16, 2016

Paul, Zachary. "Looking Back on Bette Davis' Feud with Master of Horror Larry Cohen." *Bloody-Digusting.com*. April 28, 2017.

Price, Michael H. "Moviemaker Revisits His 60s Fright-Film Salad Days in "Matinee'." *Star Tribune*. February 13, 1993.

Staff. "The Gimmicks of William Castle." T*he Times-Picayune*. February 6, 1993.

Thompson, Howard. "Thriller Double Bill." *New York Times*. July 22, 1965.

Weiner, Mitzi. "Actress Laurene Landon: "For every door that slams shut, have faith in yourself and believe that two more will open. Never give up. Never allow someone to tell you you're not good enough." *Authority Magazine*. June 28, 2019.

Yarrow, Andrew. "Gary Merrill, Actor, Dies at 74; Worked in More Than 40 Films." *New York Times*. March 7, 1990.

Internet Sources

The Internet Movie Database, www.imdb.com

Wikipedia, www.wikipedia.org

The Numbers - Box Office Data, Movie Stars, Idle Speculation, www.the-numbers.com

Box Office Mojo, www.boxofficemojo.com

John William Law is a journalist and author who has been researching and writing about film history for 25 years. First working as a reporter for weekly, monthly, and daily news publications, his first book, *Curse of the Silver Screen* was published in 1999. Since then he has written about actors, directors, filmmaking, and Hollywood history. His 2012 book, *What Ever Happened to Mommie Dearest?* Chronicled Joan Crawford's foray into horror and was published in time for the 50th anniversary of the release of *What Ever Happened to Baby Jane?* His book, *Who Nuked the Duke?* was named the best general non-fiction title at the

San Francisco Book Festival. His 2016 book, *Movie Star and the Mobster* was named best performing arts title in the Hollywood, New York, and London Book Festivals and his 2021 book *The Longest Suicide in Hollywood - The Death of Montgomery Clift* was a finalist in the International Book Awards.

In 2023, he appeared in the feature film documentary, *Conqueror: Hollywood Fallout*, which is in part inspired by his book *Who Nuked the Duke?* He has also authored two books on *Alfred Hitchcock - Alfred Hitchcock: The Icon Years* in 2010 and *The Lost Hitchcocks* in 2018, and appeared in the 2012 Universal Pictures documentary *Hitchcock's Monster Movie* for the Blu-Ray release of *The Birds*.

Milton Keynes UK
Ingram Content Group UK Ltd.
UKHW051231270324
440232UK00006B/85